CULTURES OF THE WORLD
El Salvador

Cavendish
Square

New York

Published in 2016 by Cavendish Square Publishing, LLC
243 5th Avenue, Suite 136, New York, NY 10016
Copyright © 2016 by Cavendish Square Publishing, LLC

Third Edition

This publication represents the opinions and views of the author based on his or her personal experience, knowledge, and research. The information in this book serves as a general guide only. The author and publisher have used their best efforts in preparing this book and disclaim liability rising directly or indirectly from the use and application of this book.
CPSIA Compliance Information: Batch #CW16CSQ
All websites were available and accurate when this book was sent to press.

Cataloging-in-Publication Data

Foley, Erin.
El Salvador / by Erin Foley, Rafiz Hapipi, and Debbie Nevins.
p. cm. — (Cultures of the world)
Includes index.
ISBN 978-1-5026-0808-6 (hardcover) ISBN 978-1-5026-0809-3 (ebook)
1. El Salvador — Juvenile literature. I. Foley, Erin, 1967-. II. Hapipi, Rafiz. III. Nevins, Debbie. IV. Title.
F1483.2 F65 2016
972.84—d23

Writers, Erin Foley, Rafiz Hapipi; Debbie Nevins, third edition
Editorial Director, third edition: David McNamara
Editor, third edition: Debbie Nevins
Art Director, third edition: Jeffrey Talbot
Designer, third edition: Jessica Nevins
Production Manager, third edition Jennifer Ryder-Talbot
Picture Researcher, third edition: Jessica Nevins

PRECEDING PAGE
The Izalco volcano is seen from Cerro Verde National Park near Santa Ana, El Salvador.

Printed in the United States of America

CONTENTS

EL SALVADOR TODAY

EL SALVADOR IS MORE FAMOUS FOR ITS VIOLENCE THAN FOR its beauty or its culture. This is unfortunate because this small Central American nation has breathtaking natural beauty and a vibrant, colorful culture. The capital city San Salvador is a modern city of grand boulevards and charming side streets, monuments, museums, outdoor markets, top end restaurants, and a lively nightlife. El Salvador's sandy Pacific Ocean beaches, rainforests, and dramatic volcanoes make the country a sure tourist attraction, if only tourists would come—and they have.

Since peace accords ended the country's brutal civil war in 1992, tourism has indeed been increasing, building to a high of 1,385,000 visitors in 2008. However, the amount of money tourists brought into the country continued to climb until 2013, the latest figure available at this writing. At that point, the future of El Salvador's tourism industry—as well as the country's future as a whole, perhaps—looked promising.

After all, a civilian government had been established in 1992 and had achieved a level of democratic functioning with peaceful national elections every five years. In

2009, president Mauricio Funes launched a major health reform initiative to provide universal health coverage, a move that has helped to improve the lives of poor people. The country's economy was growing, albeit slowly, and the manufacturing sector, in particular, was doing quite well.

In the 1990s and 2000s, some destructive earthquakes and hurricanes took their toll on the recovering country, knocking it down just as it was trying to get stronger. However, those natural disasters would not be El Salvador's biggest deterrent to progress.

In June 2015 the US State Department issued a frighteningly detailed travel warning to US citizens planning to go to El Salvador. The governments of the United Kingdom, Australia, and Canada likewise issued high-alert travel warnings based on El Salvador's sky-rocketing rates of crime and violence. Tourism companies, meanwhile, downplay the risk and assure potential vacationers that the nation's exploding gang warfare is not aimed at tourists and that visitors can feel completely safe if they stick to safe areas and exercise the usual travel cautions. How the dueling advice will affect tourism remains to be seen.

For the people of El Salvador, of course, life is not a vacation in a tropical paradise. They are trying to build a country on the ashes of a turbulent history of dictatorship, repression, and finally, civil war. The war lasted from 1980 to 1992. It was a conflict between the military-led, US-backed government of El Salvador, which was widely supported by the country's wealthy elite and the leaders of the Catholic Church (with some notable exceptions), and a coalition of left-wing guerrilla rebel groups, which mainly represented the poor. The

United Nations reports that more than seventy-five thousand civilians were killed and an unknown number were "disappeared," the term used to describe people who were taken away by government forces and never seen again.

Although the UN-brokered peace accords put El Salvador on the path to reconciliation, problems remain. For one thing, an amnesty law passed by the Salvadoran legislature in the wake of the peace agreement has prevented anyone from being prosecuted for the war crimes and atrocities that came to characterize the conflict. Although the UN Truth Commission found both sides to be guilty of these crimes, it concluded that the military government, with its death squads and other shadowy paramilitary groups, to be by far the greater perpetrator. This impunity, or exemption from punishment, means no one is being held responsible for the deaths of thousands of innocent people, including children. While some might argue that this amnesty allows the country to make a clean break from the past, it also has the effect of leaving matters unsettled, which often makes for an unsettled and uneasy society.

To be sure, "unsettled and uneasy" describes El Salvador today. Other factors are also at play. Although the repressive military government was dismantled, other underlying causes of the war have not been not addressed. Tremendous inequity in the distribution of wealth and land continue. No doubt this factor contributes to the recent rise in violence.

Gang warfare has made El Salvador one of the most dangerous countries on Earth. In June 2015—just one month—677 people were murdered in a country with a population of just over six million. Almost as many were killed

A worker points to a sign welcoming tourists to the "Route of Peace" in the town of Osiacala.

Police frisk men believed to be members of the MS-13 gang in Ilopango, El Salvador

in the months before that, and again in the months following—leading to a daily average homicide rate of about twenty-seven. As of August 2015, more than three hundred gang members had been killed by police and forty-four police officers had been killed.

Ironically, perhaps, this violence can be traced to the some of the same people who fled the country's earlier violence. El Salvador's most notorious gangs, Mara Salvatrucha, also known as MS-13, and Barrio 18, got their start on the streets of Los Angeles. In the early 1980s, Salvadoran immigrants escaping their country's civil war formed the gangs to defend themselves against the city's Mexican-American and African-American gangs. In the 1990s, the United States deported a large number of Salvadoran gang members, who then continued the Los Angeles street wars in Central America. MS-13 and Barrio 18 members fought each other for control of the local drug trade, extortion rackets, and other kinds of organized crime. Even so, the murder rates might not be as high, but gang members also kill their rivals simply to raise their status within their own gang. This, of course, just increases the bloodshed.

The gang members are mostly men from very poor communities. A police study in El Salvador found that just in the few blocks of San Salvador's historic center, gangs earned $100,000 a day extorting businesses, a vast sum in this poor country. That kind of money, in a country offering little opportunity to the vast number of people living in poverty, easily attracts new recruits.

An earlier truce, negotiated by the government, fell apart in 2012. The current government, under President Salvador Sánchez Cerén (2014–), has said it has no intention of negotiating with criminals and is taking a hardline approach. In the spring of 2015, he deployed heavily armed military brigades to guard El Salvador's streets. (Some people find this surprising, given that Sánchez Cerén served as a top rebel commander during the civil war.)

In August 2015, the Supreme Court of El Salvador designated the country's street gangs and those who finance them as "terrorist" organizations. Accordingly, gang members could now be charged under anti-terrorism laws, which carry longer prison sentences. Terrorism charges carry maximum penalties of up to sixty years, compared to up to twenty years for homicide or up to fifty years for aggravated homicide. It also means the government is looking to an increasingly militarized security solution. Some critics, while agreeing that the violence needs an immediate solution, worry that the constitutional rights of citizens will be trampled in the process. Some people say the gangs are operating as a shadow government, and there's no sign that the severe official government crackdown is doing any good. Some even think the country is on the path to another civil war.

Soldiers of the Special Reaction Forces train at a military base in Ilopango. The battalion was formed at the request of President Salvador Sánchez Cerén.

GEOGRAPHY

El Salvador's dramatic landscape is dominated by volcanoes.

ONLY SLIGHTLY LARGER THAN THE state of Massachusetts, El Salvador is the smallest country in Central America. However, it is more densely populated than any of its Central American neighbors. Bordered by Guatemala to the west, Honduras to the north and east, and the Pacific Ocean to the south, the landscape is dominated by two parallel east-west mountain ranges that divide the country into its three main regions: the northern mountains and plain, the central region, and the southern coastal lowlands. El Salvador is a beautiful tropical land of ruined temples and ancient Mayan cities, volcanoes, mountain lakes, and Pacific black-sand beaches.

1

El Salvador is the only Central American country with no coastline on the Caribbean Sea.

TOPOGRAPHY

It is hard to go anywhere in El Salvador without seeing a volcano. Scattered along the central region and interspersed with large, open

This view of San Salvador shows the San Vicente volcano (also called Chichontepec) on the horizon.

plateaus is a chain of twenty volcanoes. These volcanoes, several of which are still active, have played a fundamental role in the country's history and development.

It is no accident that there is a major town at the base of each of the highest volcanoes—Santa Ana, San Vicente, San Miguel, and San Salvador—all towering 6,000 to 8,000 feet (1,830 to 2,438 meters) above sea level. The volcanoes feed the land below with a mixture of ash, lava, and sediment that has made the soil extremely fertile and able to support large concentrations of people for thousands of years. Though the central region makes up only a quarter of El Salvador's land, the region contains the country's biggest cities and most of the population.

The central highlands slope down to the south to a narrow strip of land along the Pacific coast. The lowland soil is enriched by runoff from numerous small rivers that drain from the central highlands. High temperatures year-round, in addition to heavy rains, ensure that the land is thick with foliage and good for agriculture.

North of the central region is a broad plain and a band of mountains, where agricultural conditions are less ideal. Lying only 1,300 to 2,000 feet (396 to 610 m) above sea level, the plain suffers from poor drainage and acidic soil, while the steep slopes of the Sierra Madre running along the border with Honduras suffer from excessive clearing of forests and many years of overfarming.

The San Miguel volcano (also called Chaparrastique) spews ash and smoke on December 29, 2013.

A LAND OF EARTHQUAKES AND VOLCANOES

El Salvador lies in a precarious position, directly at the meeting place of three tectonic plates that cause frequent earthquakes and volcanic eruptions as they rub against each other. Although the movement of each of these tectonic plates is a barely perceptible 6 inches (15 centimeters) per year or less, over long periods of time it is enough to create chains of volcanic ridges and earthquake fault lines.

Earthquakes completely destroyed El Salvador's capital city twice, in 1756

The Izalco volcano is located in the western region of El Salvador. Its earliest recorded eruption was in 1700. It erupted regularly and was nicknamed the Lighthouse of the Pacific. At night the molten lava running down its sides turned the volcano into a brightly glowing beacon that could be seen from miles out to sea. Now black and bare, Izalco is still classified as an active volcano, but it has not erupted since 1966. The volcano stands at a height of about 6,004 feet (1,830 m).

and 1854, and badly damaged it several times in the last century. In 1986, in the midst of the civil war, an earthquake killed over a thousand people. Between January and February 2001, a series of earthquakes and thousands of aftershocks hit El Salvador. On January 13 an earthquake that measured 7.6 on the Richter scale took more than a thousand lives, while exactly a month later another earthquake killed about four hundred people. Many more were injured or left homeless. In the summer of that year, a severe drought destroyed 80 percent of the nation's crops. While the 2001 earthquakes were still fresh on peoples' minds, there was another on December 13, 2004. Thousands of Salvadorans left their homes in panic. Fortunately there were no reported casualties, and only the telephone lines were affected.

Volcanoes, too, have brought destruction to many Salvadoran towns. El Salvador has twenty-three active volcanoes. The twin-peaked San Salvador volcano, which towers above the country's capital, has not erupted since 1917. However, the town of San Miguel has suffered ten eruptions in the last century from its namesake volcano. Also called Chaparrastique volcano, the San Miguel volcano is considered one of the most active, with twenty-six eruptions in the last five hundred years, most recently in 2010 and 2013. The Santa Ana volcano erupted in October 2005, killing at least two people. Despite their destructive nature, volcanoes have been a blessing for El Salvador, making the soil extremely fertile and providing an alternative energy source in the form of geothermal energy.

RIVERS AND LAKES

El Salvador has more than three hundred rivers, and the Lempa River is the largest. It enters El Salvador in the northwest and runs for 145 miles (235 kilometers) across the country before flowing into the Pacific Ocean. The Lempa was once a major navigation and transportation route, but its importance now lies in its hydroelectric dams, the Cerrón Grande and the Cinco de Noviembre. The power harnessed by these dams helps El Salvador reduce its dependence on imported petroleum. The two dams have created lakes, adding to the natural and volcanic lakes the country already has.

Many of the volcanic craters in the central region have flooded to form beautiful lakes bordered by steep, green slopes. The largest of these is Lake Ilopango, which is located just east of San Salvador, and Lake Coatepeque in the west. Both are popular recreation spots for Salvadorans.

Lake Coatepeque is a large crater lake in Santa Ana.

A cow grazes in Usulután during a drought in July 2015. This would normally be the rainy season.

CLIMATE

Lying close to the Equator, El Salvador experiences little variation in temperature throughout the year, and seasons are marked more by the difference in levels of rainfall. Temperatures do, however, vary between the three main regions, due to differences in altitude.

The rainy season, known as *invierno* (in-vee-AIR-noh), or winter, lasts from May through October. During these months, it usually rains every evening, often in a downpour. June is the wettest month. The average total annual rainfall during *invierno* is about 80 inches (203 cm).

The dry season, known as *verano* (vay-RAH-noh), or summer, is from November through April, during which time much of El Salvador is dry and dusty. The hottest months are March and April.

The moderate climate of the central region is typified by San Salvador: at 2,156 feet (657 m) above sea level, the capital's temperature ranges from 60 degrees Fahrenheit to 94°F (16 degrees Celsius to 34°C). The coastal lowlands are usually much hotter, with an average of 83°F (28°C) and high humidity. Northern mountain areas average only 64°F (18°C), and temperatures occasionally drop to near freezing.

THE PLACE WHERE SOULS ARE CONSUMED

Archaeologists have unearthed remains of ancient cities at Tazumal and San Andrés proving that the Maya, one of the world's great civilizations, inhabited this region as far back as 5000 BCE.

Tazumal, in the Mayan language Quiché, means "pyramid where the victims were burned" or "place where souls are consumed," depending on the translation. It was an important Mayan settlement for about a thousand years until about 1200 CE. The ruins are a complex of buildings all facing west, and include tombs, pyramids, temples, and a water drainage system. It has a stepped pyramid as well as the remains of a large courtyard used for ritual ball games.

The clay vessels, ritual ornaments, and sculptures found at the ruins demonstrate that the Maya engaged in trade with people from as far away as Panama and Mexico. Efforts to uncover the wonders of the Mayan civilization started in the late nineteenth century. However, Tazumal has only been partially excavated because much of the 10-square-mile (6,400-square-acre) site is buried under the present-day town of Chalchuapa.

San Andrés, just west of San Salvador, was inhabited by a succession of Maya, Aztec, and Pipil Indians. Pottery, grinding stones, and flint have been found, and a courtyard has been excavated. In 1978 archaeologists discovered another ancient city at Joya de Cerén. The site was buried under 20 feet (6 m) of volcanic ash, which preserved artifacts providing clues to the inhabitants' daily lives. For this, it has been nicknamed "the Pompeii of Central America."

FLORA AND FAUNA

Palm trees and tropical fruit trees, such as coconut, mango, and tamarind, flourish in the hot, humid coastal plains, as do armadillos, iguanas, and snakes. El Salvador's birdlife includes wild ducks, white and royal herons, blue jays, and the urraca—a gray-headed, blue-breasted bird noted for its call, which resembles a scoffing laugh. Turtles, reptiles, and a wide variety of fish populate El Salvador's many rivers, lakes, and coastal waters.

Large-scale deforestation and agriculture have destroyed much of El Salvador's animal and plant life, both of which are not as rich as those found in other Central American countries. Rich stands of ebony, cedar, and mahogany once covered much of the country, but the trees were cleared to open up land for cultivation and to provide valuable wood for export. The mountainous regions are mostly grassland with some remnants of oak and pine forests. Formerly abundant species of cats and monkeys have disappeared from the mountains. Deer, pumas, coyotes, tapirs, and peccaries (wild pigs) can still be found there; however, the destruction of much of their habitat has decreased their numbers.

A wild adult tapir wades in the river.

MONTE CRISTO CLOUD FOREST

At the 7,931-foot (2,417-m) summit of Monte Cristo Mountain, near where the borders of El Salvador, Guatemala, and Honduras meet, lies El Trifinio, an international nature reserve protected by all three countries. Inside El Trifinio is the Monte Cristo cloud forest, the last vestige of rain forest in El Salvador and one of the few remaining cloud forests in Central America. A cloud forest is a tropical forest located at a high altitude and usually covered by clouds.

At Monte Cristo the oak and laurel trees grow almost 100 feet (31 m) tall, and their branches and leaves intertwine to form a canopy that is impenetrable to sunlight. With 100 percent humidity and 80 inches (203 cm) of rain a year, the forest is constantly dripping wet, creating an ideal habitat for a wide variety of exotic plants, including mushrooms, orchids, lichens, mosses, and ferns.

The cloud forest's protected microclimates also support an abundance of animal life not found elsewhere in El Salvador: spider monkeys, two-fingered anteaters, porcupines, spotted and hooded skunks, red and gray squirrels, and opossums. Monte Cristo is home to woodpeckers, nightingales, hummingbirds, white-faced quails, striped owls, and green toucans.

Like many tropical birds, the emerald toucanet is brightly colored.

An aerial view of
San Salvador

CITIES

For thousands of years, most of the people of El Salvador have chosen to live in the central plains, where the soil is rich and fertile. Spanish colonial settlements, many of them built on the sites of ancient native cities, have now become the principal cities of San Salvador, Santa Ana, and San Miguel.

San Salvador, the capital, now bustles with 568,000 people—2.4 million including the surrounding metropolitan area—accounting for more than 40 percent of the country's total population. Following a pattern that has been repeated in cities the world over, San Salvador has been a magnet for Salvadorans fleeing poverty and warfare in rural areas, but has failed to meet the increased demand for housing and jobs. The city reflects the huge gap between rich and poor in El Salvador: established, luxurious neighborhoods overlook the city from the surrounding hilltops, while shantytowns of makeshift huts made out of cardboard, tin, or mud cram the outskirts.

Santa Ana, with a metropolitan area population of half a million, is the transportation hub and urban center for the western half of the country. Its indigenous name, Cihuatehuacán, means "place of holy women." San Miguel, a lively market town of about 184,000, attracts visitors from all over the eastern half of the country.

A street view in Santa Ana

INTERNET LINKS

www.roughguides.com/article/mayan-ruins-el-salvador
"The Mayan Ruins Less Travelled: El Salvador's Forgotten History" offers beautiful photos and good information.

www.volcanolive.com/elsalvador.html
This site lists the country's volcanoes and their statistics.

earthquaketrack.com/p/el-salvador/biggest
Interactive maps provide info about the area's major earthquakes.

www.lonelyplanet.com/el-salvador/san-salvador
This travel site has an introduction to San Salvador and some of its highlights.

HISTORY

The Tazumal archaeological site near Santa Ana is a two thousand-year-old Mayan complex.

2

L IKE THE REST OF CENTRAL AMERICA, El Salvador has endured at least five hundred years of turmoil. The Spanish Conquest in 1528 began a turbulent era that continues today. Indeed, even though the times and technologies have changed tremendously since the days of the conquistadors, the essential root of the country's woes really does stretch back half a millennium. The displacement of the native people from their lands has been played out over and over again through the country's history, creating wide social and economic disparities.

Claiming the land for themselves, the Spanish pushed the native people into servitude and poverty and established the power of the oligarchy and the Roman Catholic Church. Even after independence, the landowning elite, the Catholic Church, and the military worked hand in hand to protect their power and wealth. Despite often brutal repression at the hands of the military, the peasants continued to fight against their landlessness and poverty. In 1980 rebellion escalated into civil war. Only since peace was negotiated in 1992, bringing promises of major

By the time the Spanish arrived in Central America in the sixteenth century, the native people had made agricultural advances far beyond those of Europeans.

A Mayan artifact on exhibit in the Tazumel Museum is thought to be a sacred object.

economic and social reform, has El Salvador been able to look forward to a brighter future. Already, however, that future promise has dimmed considerably.

ANCIENT CIVILIZATIONS

The true discoverers of the Americas were a group of Asian peoples who entered North America after crossing the Bering Strait, which separates the Asian and North American continents at their closest point. This started around twenty thousand to thirty-five thousand years ago, and they slowly migrated southward into Central and South America.

The Olmecs, who arrived around 2000 BCE, were the first ancient civilization to leave their mark in Central America. Although much about their culture remains a mystery, they are known to have made technical, artistic, and scientific advances that laid the groundwork for the extraordinary cultural achievements of the Maya.

The Maya settled in villages around 1500 BCE. Guatemala was the center of their civilization, but they also lived in the western half of El Salvador. The Maya built their economy around agriculture, cultivating an enormous variety of plants. In addition to corn, they raised beans, gourds, squash, and other produce unknown in Europe at the time, such as pineapples, tomatoes, peanuts, green peppers, cacao, vanilla, avocados, and chili peppers.

As they developed more and more advanced systems of producing food, the Maya were able to devote more time and energy to developing their skills in the arts and sciences. In hieroglyphic writing, astronomy, and mathematics, the Maya were far ahead of any other people in the New World.

The Mayan civilization declined after 900 CE. It was at this time that the Toltec Empire reached its peak of power and prosperity. The Nahuatl-speaking Toltecs disappeared around the twelfth century, opening the way

A Nahua Pipil dancer celebrates on International Day of the World's Indigenous Peoples in San Salvador.

for the Chichimec peoples. The Aztecs were among the first Chichimec peoples to move in from the north to occupy the region.

The Pipil, a Nahua people closely related to the Aztecs, are thought to have migrated south from Mexico. Around the eleventh century, the Pipil nation covered parts of what is now El Salvador and Guatemala. They called their new land Cuscatlán, or Land of the Jewel. By the time of the Spanish Conquest in the sixteenth century, there was a large class of artisans and specialists, including carpenters, potters, stonemasons, hunters, dancers, and musicians, who enjoyed a position of high honor and responsibility. Society was highly organized, with a strict hierarchy (priests, warriors, and bureaucrats occupied the top rungs of the ladder) and a well-developed government and judicial system. Books made from bark were used to record calendars, astronomical tables, taxes, dynastic history, and court records. Religion was the major focus of Nahua culture, and priests played a key role in the daily life of the people.

A painting of Pedro de Alvarado shows him attired in typical early-sixteenth century Spanish finery.

THE SPANISH CONQUEST

Hungry for gold and silver, the Spanish conquistador Pedro de Alvarado first attacked Cuscatlán in June 1524. The Pipil proved to be formidable opponents, however, and Alvarado's men were forced to withdraw to Guatemala. The Spaniards returned and finally succeeded in defeating the Pipil in 1528. They renamed the small colony El Salvador, or "The Savior," but were disappointed to find little gold or silver there.

The Spanish settlers who followed realized that El Salvador's wealth lay in the richness of its soil and the size of its native population. Knowing that huge profits could be reaped by cultivating single crops for export, the Spanish Crown took the land away from the native people and parceled it out to a handful of settlers. These settlers were popularly known as the "Fourteen Families," although the actual number was higher. They created enormous plantations to grow crops, such as cacao (for chocolate), indigo (a natural dye), and later, coffee. They then looked to the natives for labor.

The indigenous people, deprived of their livelihood, found themselves forced to work on the plantations under slave-like conditions, serve in the Spanish army, and pay monetary tributes to the local authorities. Many natives rose up in protest, but their machetes were no match for the Spaniards' guns.

INDEPENDENCE

The colonists in Central America declared their independence from Spain on September 15, 1821. Two years later, they attempted to create a confederation of states—similar to the United States of America—by forming a union called the United Provinces of Central America, but ideological differences between

In 1833, Anastasio Aquino, a native person whose brother had been imprisoned by a wealthy planter, led the most famous of many revolts against the Spanish colonists. He rallied native and mestizo peasants to protest against the government and the forced conscription of farm workers.

The strength and unity of the month-long uprising posed a serious threat to the government, but the native people were soon defeated by the heavy cannons of the government forces. Aquino was captured and executed, but he is remembered as a national hero today.

the state governments caused the confederation to fall apart. El Salvador finally declared its independence as a sovereign country in January 1841.

Independence failed to bring about any improvement to the everyday lives of most Salvadorans. The government eliminated the last communal indigenous farms and introduced anti-vagrancy laws that prevented native people from looking for new land and forced them to work for the large landowners. The landowners functioned like feudal lords, essentially making the native people into serfs.

In this painting, crowds rejoice on the day of El Salvador's independence in 1841.

LA MATANZA

La Matanza, or "The Slaughter" of 1932 is one of the great tragedies in El Salvador's history and was an early sign of the lengths to which the oligarchy was prepared to go in order to preserve their wealth and power.

The year 1931 was a time of economic hardship. The Great Depression abroad caused a sharp drop in prices for coffee, El Salvador's main export crop, and the plight of the already poor native peasants became even worse when wages and employment levels tumbled further. The creation of a Salvadoran Communist party by university student Augustín Farabundo Martí made the establishment nervous. In December 1931, the military deposed President Arturo Araújo, who was elected to his post the year before but faced rejection by the elite because of the social reforms he proposed. The military installed his vice-president, General Maximiliano Hernández Martínez, in his place.

Farabundo started agitating for change, and in January 1932 indigenous insurgents in several rural areas rose against the system of land ownership that had impoverished them. Military forces quickly suppressed the rebel forces and executed Farabundo. Intent on deterring any further protests, government soldiers systematically killed thousands of peasants and native people who had not even participated in the uprising. Estimates of the number who died range from fifteen thousand to thirty thousand.

REBELLION AND REPRESSION

La Matanza failed to prevent the continued and mounting pressure for political and economic reforms. In the 1960s, representatives from the government, the opposition, and labor and business groups recommended the large-scale redistribution of land to the farmers. Conservative members of the government, the military, and the landowning elite, however, refused to have anything to do with reform. The conservative forces reasserted their power by rigging the presidential election in 1972.

When it appeared that the victor was José Napoleón Duarte, the moderate, reformist candidate from the Christian Democratic Party, he was arrested and exiled. Social unrest and political violence began to increase. Guerrilla

THE EL MOZOTE MASSACRE

In early December 1981, the Salvadoran army's US-trained Atlacatl Battalion, led by Lieutenant Colonel Domingo Monterrosa Barrios, carried out one of the largest massacres in modern Latin American history. In the mountain villages of El Mozote, Los Toriles, La Joya, Jocote Amarillo, Rancheria, and Cerro Pando, Monterrosa and his men killed an estimated one thousand people. The massacre was named after the largest village in which it took place.

The killings were part of an army operation, called Operation Rescue, to break the guerrilla strongholds in the northern mountain region of Morazán. Although El Mozote itself was not reputed to be a guerrilla town, it was in the heart of what the army referred to as the Red Zones. Soldiers carried out a sweep of the entire area. In some villages they executed only people they believed to be guerrilla sympathizers, but in El Mozote and surrounding hamlets they killed everyone. The bodies were left as they were and the buildings set on fire.

Although eyewitness reports soon reached the outside world, Salvadoran and US officials denied that a massacre had taken place. The US Congress was in the middle of debating whether to cut off aid to El Salvador. The US government could not send aid to countries whose governments violated human rights, so the Reagan administration

A monument to the victims of the El Mozote massacre now stands in the village.

claimed that the Salvadoran government was making progress on human rights in order to be able to continue its policy of fighting Communism in El Salvador.

groups grew larger and bolder, and mass demonstrations and strikes became more frequent, all of which prompted increasingly brutal suppression by the military against anyone who was even suspected of being a subversive.

The United States wanted to support the battle against popular movements in Central America, which the United States saw as Marxist-based. Honduras was a center for this battle.

Death squads, funded by the oligarchy and organized

Government soldiers patrol a village in northern El Salvador during the civil war.

by the military, kidnapped, tortured, and killed thousands of civilians that supported or were thought to support reform. The victims were snatched away suddenly and usually never seen alive again. They came to be known as *Los Desaparecidos*, or "The Disappeared," as knowledge of their abduction, whereabouts, and fate was denied by the authorities.

CIVIL WAR

Late 1979 and early 1980 was a crucial time in El Salvador's history. Reformist young officers deposed President Carlos Humberto Romero. They set up a coalition junta that pledged sweeping land reforms and an end to repression. José Napoleón Duarte returned from exile, and hopes for a new and improved El Salvador ran high. Inevitably, however, the junta faced strong opposition from both the guerrillas and the right wing factions of the army, and death squad activity increased.

Catholic priests and nuns began to speak out against the repression and poverty, and they too became government targets. Archbishop Oscar Arnulfo

US policy in El Salvador sought to prevent a leftist or communist takeover and to try to support a moderate alternative to military rule by the junta. The United States had supplied large amounts of military and economic aid to help the Salvadoran government fight the rebel forces and support agrarian reform. Although it stopped short of sending US combat troops, the United States played a significant role in training Salvadoran army battalions, and it supplied the latest in weaponry.

Although Democratic president Jimmy Carter threatened to cut off aid in response to human rights abuses in El Salvador, he was not prepared to take the blame for any advance of Communism that a rebel victory might bring, and so concentrated instead on using military aid and social programs to encourage democracy in El Salvador. His attempts to break the oligarchy and redistribute wealth, however, only strengthened the repressive Salvadoran armed forces.

When Ronald Reagan came to power, the Republican administration called for a strengthening of the US stand against Communism in El Salvador. Around the time that initial reports of the El Mozote massacre were making front-page news in the United States, aid to El Salvador was increased. The Republicans argued that the tolerance of human rights atrocities was deplorable but necessary, because they believed a Communist victory was by far the worst disaster that could befall human rights in Central America. Preserving the Salvadoran government and helping it win the war were of paramount importance.

The Reagan policy on El Salvador failed, and the Bush administration changed it when it came into office by supporting UN efforts for peace negotiations in El Salvador. Later the Clinton administration followed in the same vein by reducing aid to El Salvador and insisting that the Salvadoran government observe the 1992 peace accord terms.

The proliferation of anti-US graffiti is evidence that many Salvadorans saw the role of the United States as interventionist and resented it. "Be a patriot, kill a Yankee" and "Imperialists, get out of El Salvador" are typical slogans.

THE TRUTH COMMISSION

Once the civil war in El Salvador came to an end, the facts were murky. What exactly had occurred and who was responsible? Lies, rumors, and cover-ups on all sides obscured the truth and hampered the processes of justice and reconciliation. In 1992, the United Nations established the Truth Commission for El Salvador to investigate human rights abuses during the war. The creation of the commission was written into the Chapultepec Peace Accords.

The commission interviewed thousands of victims and gathered evidence from many thousands of others. A team from the world-renowned Argentine Forensic Anthropology Unit (EAAF) excavated in El Mozote and found hundreds of skulls, bones, and US weapons and ammunition.

In 1993, the commission published its findings in a report titled *From Madness to Hope: the 12-year war in El Salvador.* It concluded that a massacre of over a thousand civilians had indeed occurred at El Mozote and that government-backed death squads were responsible. (In 2011, the Salvadoran government officially apologized for the massacre.) In light of the findings, the Clinton administration publicly changed the US government's stand that the massacre had not happened. The report also found that the death squads and the Salvadoran Army were behind the murder of Archbishop Óscar Romero, six Jesuit priests, the four American nuns, and thousands of civilians. The guerrilla rebels, for their part, were found guilty of murdering mayors and other members of the

The Monument to Memory and Truth in San Salvador

government, as well as other murders, kidnappings, bombings, and rapes.

As soon as the commission's report was released, the El Salvador government immediately approved an amnesty law forgiving everyone involved.

Romero was assassinated on March 24, 1980, while saying Mass. Later that year, four churchwomen from the United States were raped and killed by the military as they were driving through the countryside.

Full-scale civil war between the rebels and government forces erupted. The United States believed the rebels were supported by communist nations and feared the spread of Communism in Central America, so it supplied economic and military aid to El Salvador. José Napoleón Duarte was elected president in 1984, but his inability to bring an end to the fighting, coupled with corruption within his party, caused his downfall. The turmoil and destruction caused by the ongoing war affected every aspect of life in El Salvador, and by the late 1980s, the country's social, economic, and political problems had reached crisis proportions.

The Farabundo Martí National Liberation Front (in Spanish *Frente Farabundo Martí para la Liberación Nacional*), or FMLN, was formed on October 10, 1980, as an umbrella group of several leftist guerrilla organizations that had participated in the Salvadoran Civil War. After peace accords were signed in 1992, all armed FMLN units were demobilized and their organization became a legal political party. The FMLN is now one of the two major political parties in El Salvador.

A twelve-year-old guerrilla of the FMLN holds an M16 rifle during the war in 1989.

Salvador Sánchez Cerén of the FMLN party celebrates his victory in the 2014 presidential election.

PEACE

In the late 1980s, international pressure to end the war increased. Negotiations between the government and the FMLN guerrillas began in September 1989 but were disrupted by further violence. The FMLN attempted a final offensive to overthrow the Salvadoran government, but failed to rouse enough popular support. The army, for its part, broke into the University of Central America in San Salvador and murdered six Jesuit priests, their housekeeper, and her daughter. These killings shocked international observers as well as people in El Salvador. US aid was halted, and both the government and the FMLN invited the United Nations to mediate.

After two years of hard negotiating, a peace agreement was finally signed in January 1992. Under the terms of the Chapultepec Peace Accords, the FMLN became a legal political party. It agreed to lay down its arms in return for wide-ranging reforms, including land redistribution, a substantial decrease in the size and role of the armed forces, and a purge of the worst human rights offenders from the army officer corps. The agreement also called for a 70 percent reduction in the size of the nation's armed forces and the dissolution of the National Police and other forces.

ACHIEVING DEMOCRACY

By 2004 FMLN and the Nationalist Republican Alliance (Spanish: *Alianza Republicana Nacionalista*), or ARENA, a rightist political party, were the largest political parties. Both parties enjoyed political success throughout the first decade of the twenty-first century. ARENA candidates won four consecutive presidential elections until the election of Mauricio Funes of the FMLN in March 2009. Allegations of rampant corruption in the administration of the previous president, Antonio "Tony" Saca (served 2004–2009), played a role in the outcome of the 2009 election. Saca ended up being expelled by his own ARENA party, and in 2013, he was sued for corruption and money laundering.

In 2014, Salvador Sánchez Cerén, also of the FMLN, and the previous vice president, became El Salvador's new president with 50.11 percent of the vote. Cerén was a guerrilla leader in the civil war and is the first former rebel to serve as president.

The signing of the peace accord on January 16, 1992, at Chapultepec Castle in Mexico marked the end of the most violent period in El Salvador's history.

INTERNET LINKS

www.aljazeera.com/indepth/opinion/2012/02/2012228123122975116.html
An article by an American university professor presents a balanced look at the civil war atrocities.

news.bbc.co.uk/2/hi/1891145.stm
This article, from 2002, examines the "US role in Salvador's brutal war."

www.cja.org/article.php?list=type&type=199
The Center for Justice and Accountability provides an excellent explanation of the Salvadoran Civil War, with extensive sources.

www.derechos.org/nizkor/salvador/informes/truth.html
The full text of the Truth Commission's report can be found here.

www.theguardian.com/world/2015/may/22/hundreds-of-thousands-to-attend-oscar-romero-beatification-in-el-salvador
Salvadorans take a look back at the civil war as the Catholic Church honors the late Archbishop Oscar Arnulfo Romero in 2015.

GOVERNMENT

President Salvador Sánchez Cerén waves during his inauguration on June 1, 2014.

3

SINCE 1992, EL SALVADOR HAS been remaking itself into a civilian democracy—and with some success. The armed forces had long dominated political life in El Salvador, despite a constitution that describes the country as a democratic republic with an elected president.

The oligarchy and the military regularly set democracy aside, using coups, rigged elections, and repression to maintain their power and prestige. Government repression was particularly brutal during the twelve-year civil war that ended in 1992. During this period, tens of thousands of ordinary Salvadorans were harassed, tortured, or killed by government forces for speaking out in favor of reform. Killings by paramilitary death squads went not only unpunished but unacknowledged by the courts.

The 1992 peace agreement established a framework for reforming the judicial system, electoral process, armed forces, and police. Many of these changes have been highly controversial and difficult to implement, but a degree of progress has been made in some areas despite long delays.

THE MILITARY

The president of the republic is the Commander in Chief of the military. In accordance with the 1992 peace agreement, the Salvadoran military forces were largely demobilized. The Treasury Police, National Guard, and

Article 89 of El Salvador's Constitution calls for the "total or partial reconstruction of the Republic of Central America," a short-lived union of the Central American nations from 1821 to 1841. The constitutional reference appears to be merely a traditional claim of unity and solidarity with the other Central American nations.

Salvadoran soldiers take part in a ceremony in 2014.

National Police were abolished, and military intelligence functions were transferred to civilian control. By 1993, the military had cut personnel from a war-time high of sixty-three thousand to the level of thirty-two thousand required by the peace accords. By 1999, the Armed Forces numbered less than fifteen thousand, including personnel in the army, navy, and air force. A purge of military officers accused of human rights abuses and corruption was also completed in 1993 in compliance with the UN Truth Commission's recommendations. The military's new doctrine, professionalism, and complete withdrawal from political and economic affairs have transformed it into the most respected institution in El Salvador.

Today the Armed Forces of El Salvador enjoys a high approval rating among the country's citizens. It has also begun to include women soldiers. In 2011, an all female battalion of sixty-two soldiers was formed. Women also serve as helicopter and airplane pilots.

THE CONSTITUTION

The El Salvadoran government operates, at least theoretically, under the dictates of the nation's constitution. The current constitution was enacted in 1983 and amended in 2003. The document spells out the structure of the government, and lists the rights and responsibilities of citizens.

Among those rights are the right to free expression that "does not subvert the public order"; the right of free association and peaceful assembly for any legal purpose; the legal presumption of innocence; the legal inadmissibility of forced confession, and the right to the free exercise of religion—with the stipulation that it remain within the bounds of "morality and public order." Citizens age eighteen and over are also granted the right to vote. However, the constitution also states that suffrage is an obligation as well as a right.

Technically, those who do not vote are subject to a fine, but it is rarely enforced.

The document also outlines the country's economic system. It guarantees the right to private enterprise and private property. In 2003, the constitution was amended to prohibit the military from playing an internal security role except under extraordinary circumstances. This stipulation was required by the 1992 peace agreement.

NATIONAL GOVERNMENT

The government is divided into three branches: the executive, the legislative assembly, and the judiciary.

El Salvador's national coat of arms adorns the horizontal white stripe in the center of the country's flag.

THE EXECUTIVE BRANCH   This branch, consisting of the president, the council of ministers, and the undersecretaries of state, is responsible for preparing the budget, managing the armed forces and the security forces, and directing foreign relations. Presidential elections are held every five years, and presidents cannot serve more than one term of office in a row. Every presidential candidate must belong to a legally recognized political party and needs an absolute majority of the votes in order to win.

THE LEGISLATIVE ASSEMBLY   The eighty-four members of the unicameral Legislative Assembly are also popularly elected, serving renewable three-year terms. The Legislative Assembly controls taxes, sanctions the budget, and ratifies or rejects international treaties.

THE JUDICIARY The most important judicial institution is the Supreme Court of Justice. Composed of the constitutional, civil, and criminal chambers, the Supreme Court rules on the constitutionality of laws and acts as the last level of appeal in civil and criminal cases.

The cause of El Salvador's civil war was directly related to glaring disparities of wealth between the elite ruling class and the poverty-stricken majority. The military rule governing El Salvador for half a century brutally protected the status quo. Consequently, the peace accord, among other things, sought to restructure and reduce the political influence and autonomy of the armed forces. The negotiations focused on not only putting an end to the conflict, but also putting into motion three transitions simultaneously: from war to peace, from militarization to demilitarization, and from authoritarianism to democracy.

The peace accord has been most effective in reforming the armed forces, which no longer plays a part in public security. However, the new judiciary suffered from corruption and inefficiency and was staffed by unqualified personnel. The new National Civilian Police (PNC) corps was staffed with 1,500 former soldiers from the partially decommissioned army, and may still be involved in human rights violations and other criminal activities.

The peace accords were not able to adequately address the country's huge disparities of wealth, and the hope was that the democratic system would

Members of the National Civil Police search for gang members in San Salvador in 2015.

eventually sort that out. The two largest political parties, however, have opposing views on how best to deal with such problems, and regardless of which one is in power, not much has been accomplished. Therefore, the root causes of economic inequality remain.

A sharp spike in gang violence in recent years is seen as the result of these political failures. Critics charge the FMLN-backed Presidents Mauricio Funes (2009–2014) and Salvador Sánchez Cerén (2014–) with ineffectiveness in controlling the alarming, escalating gang situation. Many fear that gang warfare will soon expand into civil warfare yet again.

LOCAL GOVERNMENT

El Salvador is divided into fourteen administrative departments (equivalent to states in the United States), which in turn are divided into 261 municipalities (equivalent to counties). Each department has a governor and a substitute governor who are appointed by the government.

The citizens of each municipality directly elect their own municipal council, composed of a mayor, a legal representative, and two or more council members, depending on the population of the municipality.

POLITICAL PARTIES

There are two main political parties in El Salvador, the Nationalist Republican Alliance (ARENA), and the Farabundo Martí National Liberation Front (FMLN). Since 2000, the two parties have gone back and forth in controlling the largest number of Legislative Assembly seats.

ARENA is a right-wing party; presidents representing this party were Alfredo Cristiani (1989—1994), Armando Calderón Sol (1994—1999), Francisco Flores Pérez, (1999—2004), and Antonio Saca (2004—2009).

FMLN is a left-wing party, formed out of five political parties representing the rebels during the civil war. Presidents from this party include Mauricio Funes (2009—2014) and Salvador Sánchez Cerén (2014—).

There are also a number of smaller political parties, with the Christian Democratic Party (PDC) being the next largest.

ELECTIONS

The 1994 presidential, legislative, and municipal elections were significant in many ways. It is rare for all three elections to be held concurrently, but more importantly, they were the first to be held since civil war ended and the first to be open to the FMLN guerrilla group, which became a legal party in 1992. The elections were seen as a test of the ability of a civilian government to hold its own against the military. Although it lost the elections, FMLN established itself as the major opposition party.

STEPS TOWARD JUSTICE

More than two decades after the signing of the peace accord, many of the people responsible for abuses committed during the war have not been brought to justice. The country's 1993 Amnesty Law remains in place. It has ensured impunity for the guilty, which leaves society feeling unsettled.

Some small steps have been made toward justice. In 2013–2014, the Salvadoran Attorney General's Office reopened the investigation into the 1981 El Mozote massacre and other specific instances of mass carnage. Authorities also approved a reparations program for survivors who suffered human rights violations.

In April 2015, after a sixteen-year legal battle, the US government deported El Salvador's former defense minister, Gen. Carlos Eugenio Vides Casanova. Vides had moved to Florida in 1989 and had been living there ever since as a legal permanent resident. US immigration courts found that he had participated in torture and killings by troops under his command. Human rights activists accuse Vides of involvement in the 1980 murders of

A human rights activist takes part in a demonstration demanding justice for the victims of massacres during the civil war.

four American churchwomen. The former general's deportation signaled a complete about-face for US government policy toward Central America.

The US Justice Department also began proceedings against another former Salvadoran military officer, Col. Inocente Orlando Montano Morales. He is facing charges in Spain in the 1989 killings in San Salvador of five Spanish Jesuit priests.

Since then, elections have continued according to plan and the office of president has passed peacefully every five years. Until 2009, ARENA won four presidencies in a row. FMLN won its first presidential election in 2009 and again in 2014. The next presidential election is to be held in February 2019.

A man casts his vote during legislative and municipal elections in San Salvador in 2015.

INTERNET LINKS

web.archive.org/web/20150103200933/http://confinder.richmond.edu/admin/docs/ElSalvador1983English.pdf
Here you can find the full text of the El Salvador Constitution in English.

www.cia.gov/library/publications/the-world-factbook/geos/es.html
The CIA World Factbook has up-to-date information on El Salvador's government.

topics.nytimes.com/top/news/international/countriesandterritories/elsalvador/index.html
The New York Times offers its most recent articles about El Salvador along with links to other sources.

sansalvador.usembassy.gov
The site of the US Embassy in El Salvador.

www.state.gov/r/pa/ei/bgn/2033.htm
The US Department of State Fact Sheet on El Salvador.

ECONOMY

A Salvadoran man prepares to go to work at dawn in La Libertad, a tourist center and an important fishing village on the Salvadoran coast.

4

ALTHOUGH EL SALVADOR IS THE smallest country in Central America, it has the fourth largest economy. For thousands of years, that economy was based on agriculture, but that's no longer the case. Today, agriculture accounts for only 10 percent of the economy's productivity, though 21 percent of the labor force works in that sector.

The apparel industry has grown in recent years to be El Salvador's leading export sector. In 2012, the largest single export product, accounting for 16 percent of trade, was T-shirts.

A man cleans plantains to be sold in Chatatenango.

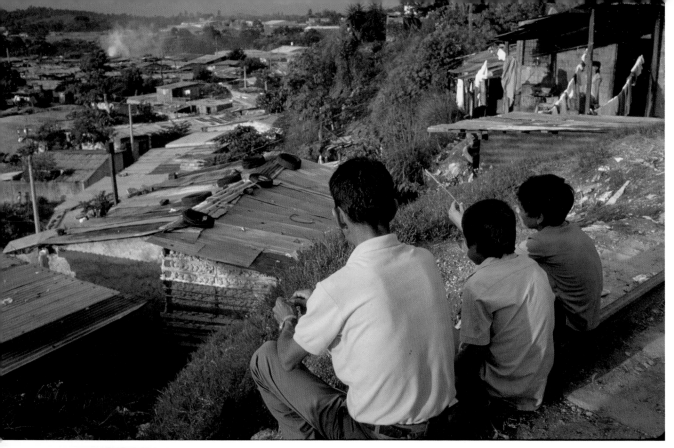

Boys sit on a hillside above the roofs of shacks in a poor neighborhood.

Centuries ago, when the Spanish colonists pushed the indigenous people off their small communal farms and used the land to grow cash crops, they made a fundamental change to the economy. Cash crops were indeed a success, and the later diversification into a greater variety of crops and into manufacturing ensured continued high levels of economic growth and extreme wealth for the few large landowners. The uneven distribution of wealth resulted in long-term political instability and, eventually, civil war. The war, in turn, had a major impact on the economy, causing a massive outflow of money, the destruction of much of the country's infrastructure, a decrease in exports, investment, and consumption, and even higher levels of unemployment. The peace accord brought generous foreign aid and the return of capital from abroad, restoring economic growth.

Despite economic growth and relative stability, 36.5 percent of the population still lives below the poverty line. Economic benefits have not been evenly shared across the different levels of the population.

COFFEE

Coffee has a long history that is shrouded in legend. First cultivated about 575 CE, it was not grown extensively until the fifteenth century. By the sixteenth and seventeenth centuries, coffee consumption had spread throughout Persia and Turkey, continental Europe, England, and America. Europeans were in love with the drink. Coffeehouses sprang up everywhere and became popular social, literary, and political gathering places; King Charles II saw them as centers of dissent and tried, unsuccessfully, to shut them down.

Coffee grows wild in some parts of Ethiopia, where it originated, but is now cultivated wherever its needs for a hot and moist climate, rich soil, and a high altitude are met.

El Salvador has an ideal climate for coffee, but it was not until synthetic dyes made indigo unprofitable in the mid-1800s that the country began to direct its resources toward the large-scale production of coffee beans. This entailed putting the large peasant population to work on the plantations, laying the roads and railroads necessary for transporting the crop, and building processing plants.

In 1990 coffee prices crashed as a result of the overproduction of coffee worldwide. In 1993 El Salvador participated in the Coffee Retention Plan, which was an agreement among the world's

A man rakes coffee beans to dry in the sun.

coffee exporters to limit coffee production and thus boost prices. That, however, did not stop coffee from declining in importance in the Salvadoran economy.

Since 2000, the industry has been greatly affected by increased competition from other countries on the world market, whose cheaper coffee beans have caused prices to plummet. In response, some small- to medium-sized coffee producers are aiming instead at international higher-grade coffee markets, with many producers now cultivating shade-grown, fair trade, and organic coffees, which meet higher standards and earn higher prices.

Although coffee's role in the Salvadoran economy has diminished, it continues to provide El Salvador with a dependable export income.

LAS CATORCE FAMILIAS ("THE FOURTEEN FAMILIES")

El Salvador's power and wealth was concentrated in the hands of the Fourteen Families. They were the large landowners who functioned like feudal lords. By the end of the nineteenth century, with the expansion of the coffee industry, the group became, for all intents, an oligarchy. An oligarchy is a small group of people who are in control of a country. Strongly supported by the Catholic Church, this closely-knit group exercised its control through the government and a newly created National Guard, and thus managed to preserve its position and suppress any dissent.

Throughout the twentieth century, this entitled group controlled more than 70 percent of El Salvador's private banks, sugar mills, coffee production and exports, as well as television and newspapers. As agriculture became less important to the nation's economy, the elite moved their interests into the financial industry, creating eight large corporations that have dominated El Salvador's economy since 1989: Grupo Cuscatlán, Banagrícola, Banco Salvadoreño, Banco de Comercio, Grupo Agrisal, Grupo Poma, Grupo de Sola, and Grupo Hill.

Today, the descendants of the well-known families hold on to vast fortunes while more than one third of the nation's people live in poverty.

People wait in line for a free breakfast outside a Catholic humanitarian center in San Salvador.

AGRICULTURE

El Salvador's wealth was built on the export of just three crops: cacao, indigo, and coffee. This reliance on monocrops could not continue, however, as it made the Salvadoran economy extremely vulnerable to fluctuations in the economies of its trading partners. El Salvador diversified its agricultural exports into cotton, sugar, corn, rice, sorghum, beans, oilseed, and beef and dairy products.

The structure of the Salvadoran economy has changed considerably, and in 2014 agriculture as a whole accounted for only 10 percent of the country's GDP. This is in contrast to the situation in 1987, when it made up 25 percent of the GDP. Nevertheless, agriculture is still an important component of the economy and provides employment to 21 percent of the labor force.

A worker fills a bag with coffee beans at a facility in El Paste.

LAND REFORM Landlessness is a historical source of unrest in El Salvador. Many attempts to redistribute land from the few large landowners to the majority of landless peasants have ended either in failure or in very limited partial success, contributing to the country's long history of poverty and violence.

Land reform was a key condition of the 1992 peace accord. The World Bank provided loans to El Salvador in 1996 and 2005. However, despite international financial aid, land redistribution has been slow and inefficient due to such factors as bureaucracy; the plummeting prices of cash crops, particularly coffee; bad weather; political opposition and landowner noncooperation; and regional economics.

Construction workers build a section of a new highway.

CONSTRUCTION

Since the 1992 peace accord, the return of capital, private investment, and national reconstruction programs have brought about growth in the construction industry. It was the leading sector in 2001 with a growth rate of 10 percent, due in part to the post-earthquake reconstruction projects. In the same year the construction sector employed 5.4 percent of the workforce and accounted for 3.9 percent of the GDP. However, in 2014, the industry took a hit and experienced about a 10 percent fall, critics say due to government inaction and bureaucracy holding up many projects. In addition the extreme spike in El Salvador's murder rate in 2015 naturally impacted industrial growth in the construction industry, as well as in many others.

TRANSPORTATION AND UTILITIES

During the war much of El Salvador's infrastructure was severely damaged by guerrilla forces. Peace has brought pledges of financial support from around the world for the reconstruction of major highways, power plants, electrical towers, and telecommunications facilities.

ADOPTING THE DOLLAR

In 2001, El Salvador began to phase out its own currency, the colón, and switch over to the US dollar. Ecuador had done the same the year before in order to help stabilize its high rate of inflation. According to economists, the benefits of switching to the dollar—a process called dollarization—would be to lower interest rates and stimulate investment. These developments would, in turn, stimulate trade and help to grow the economy. In addition, dollarization would accommodate the huge sum of remittances in US dollars being sent home by overseas workers. The dollar had already been an unofficial currency, coexisting with the colón, in the country for a long time.

Since the switch, the effect on El Salvador's economy hasn't been as successful as officials had hoped. The move tended to raise prices on products as producers and merchants rounded up their prices to the nearest nickel, dime, or quarter. Rounding up might not seem to make a big difference, but to the lowest-income Salvadorans, it hurt a great deal.

Although indications are that the switch did lower interest rates some, investment did not follow as hoped. For one thing, the worldwide economic crisis of 2008 caused investment panic across the board. A few years later, by 2013, violence and gang warfare began escalating so quickly in El Salvador that overseas investors often looked elsewhere for safer economic initiatives.

The new Salvadoran president, since 2014, Salvador Sánchez Cerén, has argued for de-dollarization, so the future of this policy in El Salvador remains to be seen.

Demonstrators protest against dollarization.

Mobile-cellular phone services are expanding rapidly, and in 2014, there were some 9.2 million cell phones in use, which amounts to about 150 percent of the population.

Internet connectivity is available in El Salvador, and in 2014, there were about 1.7 million Internet users, about 27 percent of the population.

El Salvador depends on imported oil for its energy needs. The country has tried to decrease its dependence on imported petroleum by developing alternative forms of energy. Renewable energy sources, such as hydroelectric plants, solid and liquid biomass, and geothermal energy provide almost half of the country's energy needs.

MANUFACTURING

El Salvador's manufacturing sector experienced rapid growth during the 1960s, but suffered a drastic decline during the 1980s when the civil war caused a shortage of capital and foreign currency, guerrilla sabotage of electrical power plants and factories, protests by labor unions, and reduced demand for products both at home and abroad. Nevertheless, the sector has

A young woman sews pajamas for Walmart in a factory outside San Salvador.

managed to get back on track. In 2014, manufacturing accounted for 25 percent of the GDP, and employed about 20 percent of the workforce. Apparel manufacturing leads the manufacturing sector's performance. Clothing and textiles, and products such as medicine, soap, iron, steel, and machinery generate more foreign earnings for El Salvador than do agricultural exports.

MONEY FROM ABROAD

El Salvador relies heavily on remittances and foreign aid, which, along with the return of private investment capital, has increased since peace was negotiated in 1992.

Driven by poverty, as many as three million Salvadorans are estimated to be living and working abroad, especially in the United States. They send money home every month. In 2014, such remittances totalled 17 percent of the Salvadoran GDP, one of the highest rates in the world. One third of all Salvadoran households were receiving those monies. Despite the large amount, remittance money is only sufficient for purchasing basic items, such as food and clothing, in El Salvador. Post-war economic policies, such as dollarization, privatization, and huge tax breaks for large corporations, have almost doubled the cost of living for the average Salvadoran. Now, more than before, Salvadorans are desperately depending on remittances by family members working abroad.

After picking up his remittance money from a relative in the United States, a man walks out of the MoneyGram office in Intipuca.

INTERNET LINKS

www.heritage.org/index/country/elsalvador
This site rates El Salvador's "economic freedom" according to its own formula to evaluate its business climate.

voiceselsalvador.wordpress.com/2011/06/08/ten-years-later-the-impact-of-dollarization-in-el-salvador
This article examines the effects of El Salvador's currency switch.

A blue heron struts in a mangrove in the Jiquilisco Bay Biosphere Reserve.

5

PROBLEMS WITH EL SALVADOR'S environment, particularly deforestation, have their roots deep in social, political, and economic inequalities, which can be traced all the way back to the colonial era. Colonists took land away from the locals and forced them to work on plantations. In successive centuries the landowning elite worked hand in hand with the authorities to ensure that the majority of the population remained landless farmers. The 1980s land reforms were unsuccessful because the farmers were given land that was infertile. The signing of peace agreements in 1992 allowed the government to refocus and better manage its heavily depleted resources. Progress, however, has been slow.

DEFORESTATION

El Salvador has lost almost 85 percent of its forest since the 1960s. Deforestation is therefore a main environmental concern for El Salvador, which now has a total forest area of 298,000 acres (120,600 hectares), or only about 5 percent of the land. The forest area declined 37 percent between 1990 and 2000 alone. Many of the forests have made way for large coffee plantations and other agricultural projects by wealthy landowners. The trees were also destroyed in the civil war or cut for firewood by rural Salvadorans. Adding to the problem are overpopulation, which means more and more land is needed for building residences, and indiscriminate slashing and burning of trees to clear farmland for cultivation.

The absence of trees leaves the topsoil vulnerable to erosion, which leaches the soil of its fertility. Deforestation also leads to a lower amount of transpiration, which dries out the air. Temperatures increase and the amount of rainfall decreases as a result. Water bodies dry up, and more

NATIONAL RECONCILIATION FOREST

Twelve years of civil war in El Salvador took more than seventy-five thousand lives and caused widespread damage. It was estimated that areas surrounding Guazapa Mountain alone were pounded with 4,000 tons (0.9 metric tons) of napalm and white phosphorus bombs. These caused huge craters in the mountainside, and the resulting fires wiped out much of the forest. By the end of the war, bare ridges and stretches of dry riverbeds replaced what used to be dense canopies of greenery and clear, flowing rivers.

In 1996 the people of Guazapa launched a project to convert much of the bare mountain soil into what was called the National Reconciliation Forest. The project involved planting seventy-five thousand trees, one for each person killed in the civil war, high on the volcanic slopes of Guazapa Mountain. On the lower slopes they planted trees for timber and fuel. To the people there, the simple logic of "more trees, more water, more animals, more fertile lands" drives them to take responsibility for helping the mountain recover. Apart from restoring the forest and rebuilding the ecosystem, the project also educates farmers on sustainable agricultural practices.

people do not have access to sufficient clean water. This, combined with declining crop yields due to the poor quality of the soil, affects Salvadorans' lives and livelihood.

The country's species biodiversity has suffered as a direct result of deforestation. Many species of plants and animals, such as the jaguar and scarlet macaw, have become extinct. Some migratory birds from North America are deprived of their transit nests in El Salvador during their journey south in the winter.

MANGROVE MANAGEMENT

Forests in the coastal areas and wetlands are not spared from exploitation. Without access to electricity, rural residents living along coastal areas cut trees in mangrove forests for firewood. Mostly shrimp farmers, these Salvadorans living in the coastal areas do not realize that the destruction of mangrove forests may affect their very livelihood. Aquatic wildlife, such as

People wash clothes and swim on the shore of the highly contaminated Lake Ilopango.

shellfish and shrimp, has been affected by the reduction in mangrove forests. There is also worry that excessive farming of shrimp may upset the ecological balance in mangroves. Mangroves are important in preventing coastal erosion and to some extent provide some protection to the coast against destructive tidal waves.

WATER CRISIS

El Salvador has less fresh water than any other country in Latin America, and what water it does have is mostly contaminated. As much as 98 percent of the country's fresh water is polluted. The reasons include deforestation, a lack of wastewater treatment facilities, and mining activities.

Deforestation dried up water supplies and caused severe soil erosion, washing soil into streams and rivers. Nearly all of El Salvador's municipal sewage—98 percent—and about 90 percent of its industrial wastewater is discharged to rivers and creeks without any treatment at all. Mining has caused dangerous chemicals to leach into groundwater and wells.

THE FIGHT AGAINST MINING

One of the few things both major parties in El Salvador appear to agree on is that it's not in the country's interest to allow large-scale mining. Most officials believe the severity of the nation's water problem trumps the jobs that the mining companies would provide. In any event, government officials agree that the decision should be El Salvador's to make. Things are not that simple, however.

In 2009, the Canadian mining company Pacific Rim obtained permits from the Salvadoran government to explore for potential mining prospects. When even those minor operations ended up contaminating wells in the region, the government denied the mining company's application to move from exploration to full-scale mining.

The mining company, now owned by the Australian firm Oceanagold, filed suit against the people and government of El Salvador for $301 million for denying the company's investors their expectation of profit. The company is suing to have this dispute heard not in the Salvadoran courts but by the World Bank's International Center for the Settlement of Investment Disputes. That would mean the ultimate decision could be made outside of El Salvador.

Fighting such a legal battle is a very expensive undertaking for El Salvador, which can ill afford it. The damages that Pacific Rim

Protestors rally against the World Bank's procedures in the Pacific Rim vs. El Salvador mining lawsuit.

is claiming equals about half of what El Salvador spends on education. Aside from the money is the question of national sovereignty, and whether a small, impoverished country can protect itself against the interests of multinational corporations.

In recent years, a number of environmental and community groups are taking a human rights approach to protect their water supplies. *El Foro del Agua* (The Water Forum), a coalition of more than a hundred organizations, is calling for a national ban on metal mining, a constitutional amendment recognizing the human right to water, and a general water law that would legally establish social control of water resources and services.

The coalition and its supporters hope these legal victories, if they are accomplished, would give El Salvador the power it needs to fight the interests of transnational corporations such as mining companies.

URBAN POLLUTION

Poverty and overpopulation remain the primary cause of environmental degradation. About 67 percent of Salvadorans live in urban areas, particularly San Salvador, Santa Ana, and San Miguel. The city of San Salvador is home to almost one-quarter of El Salvador's population.

A woman and her son pick through trash at the city dump in Apopa.

Smog obscures the view of downtown San Salvador.

Overcrowding and the absence of proper sanitation are the main culprits of air, water, and solid waste pollution. There is heavy traffic on the roads, and poorly maintained vehicles emit thick black smoke. The smoke remains in the air because it is trapped by the surrounding hills and mountains.

In terms of housing, there is still a disparity between the rich few and the poor masses. The latter live mostly in makeshift houses in areas without a municipal sewage system. They dispose of solid waste in their backyards, rivers, and streams. With the rapidly growing urban population, it is an uphill task for Salvadorans to resolve the environmental crisis.

INTERVENTION AND CONSERVATION EFFORTS

Environmental issues became a priority during the reconstruction of post-war El Salvador. A presidential decree created the Ministry of Environment and Natural Resources (MARN) in 1997 to better manage

Environmental activists march to commemorate World Water Day in San Salvador in 2014.

the country's resources. The ministry coordinates efforts by the government and non-governmental organizations (NGOs) in the area of environmental conservation. It is also responsible for recommending environmental legislation and enforcing existing ones in El Salvador. Apart from environmental rehabilitation, MARN has established the National Protected Areas System (SANP), which marks geographical areas of concern according to such categories as national parks, national monuments, habitat or species management areas, and marine and terrestrial landscapes. From 1990 to 2012, the country's designated land and marine protected areas grew from none at all to 8.69 percent of its total territorial area.

El Salvador is also involved in the Mesoamerican Biological Corridor. This is a project that seeks to protect ecosystems in the natural land bridge region between North America and South America. This includes Belize, Guatemala, El Salvador, Honduras, Nicaragua, Costa Rica, Panama, and some southern states of Mexico. The concept is to protect biodiversity by providing a unified natural corridor for species which use the bridge in migration. The project also aspires to unite the conservation efforts of the Central American nations.

Several international organizations, such as the World Bank, United Nations Environment Program (UNEP), and the Global Environment Facility, provide funding for this large and complex project. It employs a multi-pronged approach to conservation, such as relocating communities out of ecologically fragile areas. However, the project has become mired in controversy caused by distrust between the locals and corridor implementers.

International funding and participation in such projects have facilitated El Salvador's efforts in reforestation, management of natural areas, wildlife conservation, and management of solid waste. Although faced with a few setbacks, such as Hurricane Mitch in 1998 and a series of devastating earthquakes in 2001, environmental rehabilitation in El Salvador is well under way. One major challenge that the government must overcome to ensure future environmental sustainability in the long run will be the eradication of poverty and the management of overpopulation.

Volunteers plant new trees as part of a reforestation project at a zoo in **Tegucigalpa**.

INTERNET LINKS

www.aljazeera.com/indepth/ features/2011/02/201122017470922665.html
"El Salvador's Environmental Crisis" looks at how climate change and environmental problems affect the country's poor people.

policy-practice.oxfamamerica.org/work/resource-rights/protecting- the-right-to-decide
Oxfam America looks at the mining company lawsuit against El Salvador.

www.progressio.org.uk/blog/empowered-blog/el-salvador-problem- water
This article examines the country's water problem.

SALVADORANS

A skateboarder performs in El Salvador del Mundo Square in San Salvador on Go Skateboarding Day.

6

S ALVADORANS ARE LARGELY homogenous ethnically and linguistically. By far most of the country's people are *mestizo*, of mixed indigenous and Spanish descent, as is the case throughout Central America. About 86 percent of Salvadorans fall into this ethnic category. Another 12 percent of the people are mainly of white European descent. These people are mostly of Spanish descent, and less than 1 percent is primarily or only of indigenous descent.

At least 36 percent of Salvadorans live below the poverty line, and most work long hours on plantations, in factories, or in the military for very low wages. A small percentage have achieved middle-class status by becoming teachers, doctors, civil servants, or business people, or by rising through the ranks of the military.

DESCENDANTS OF THE PIPIL

The original people of what is now El Salvador were a network of Mayan tribes who inhabited the region for thousands of years. Their descendants, the Pipil, lived in the area when the Spanish arrived in the

In 2014, the Salvadoran legislature ratified an amendment of the country's constitution to officially recognize its indigenous population. Article 63 reads, "El Salvador recognizes the Indigenous Peoples and will adopt public policies that will maintain and develop their ethnic and cultural identities, their cosmic vision, values and spirituality."

A Pipil woman participates in a ceremony during International Day of the World's Indigenous Peoples in San Salvador.

sixteenth century, but disease, persecution, and intermarriage led to their gradual elimination.

Less than 1 percent of Salvadorans are descendants of the Pipil, who inhabited El Salvador before the arrival of the Spanish. Primarily Pancho and Izalco people, they live in a cluster of villages in southwestern El Salvador near the Guatemalan border. Their elaborate ceremonial costumes are reserved for special occasions, but some native women still wear a version of the traditional skirt with plain white or brightly colored blouses. Only a few elders still speak their native Nahua language. Although the government and the Jesuit-run University of Central America attempted to revive the Nahua language and customs in the 1970s, indigenous people shied away from the effort once the civil war broke out. A long history of persecution at the hands of the government and the oligarchy has resulted in many native people refusing even to teach Nahua to their children.

THE OLIGARCHY

Salvadorans of direct European descent make up only a tiny percent of the population, yet this small white minority has—directly or indirectly—controlled the country's power and wealth for five hundred years. The oligarchy's lifestyle is much the same as that of wealthy people in any other big, modern, cosmopolitan city: they wear designer clothes, drive luxury cars, and vacation abroad. Even within this elite there is a hierarchy. At the top of the pyramid are the families of the "founding fathers"—the original Spanish settlers of El Salvador; next are the descendants of the bankers and financiers who immigrated from various parts of Europe in the nineteenth and early twentieth centuries; at the bottom are the newly rich Palestinians, Lebanese, and Jews, who make up the merchant class. The upper class also includes the officer ranks of the military, although the oligarchy and military remain separate entities and tend not to mix socially.

Two Salvadoran sisters smile for the camera.

THE MIDDLE CLASS

Making up only about 16 percent of the population (this number differs according to various sources, depending on how "middle class" is defined), El Salvador's middle class includes professional and skilled workers, government employees, school teachers, and small landowners. Although the middle class has tended to encourage land reform and push for an improvement in the standard of living of most Salvadorans, they have had little direct influence in the country's affairs.

LANDLESS PEASANTS AND URBAN POOR

Whether they live in the city or in the countryside, most mestizo and native Salvadorans are poor and unemployed. They try to eke out a living by working on plantations, in factories, or in the military. Agricultural work is seasonal, so even farm workers are out of work for part of the year. Thousands of people flock to the cities each year in search of work, despite the fact that urban unemployment is high. They do whatever they can to get by, living in makeshift huts and selling fruit and vegetables on the streets.

SALVADORANS IN THE UNITED STATES

During the civil war, some two million Salvadorans fled to the United States, Mexico, and other Central American countries. About half of those sought refuge in the United States. Many refugees moved to Los Angeles, which today has the largest Salvadoran population in the country. Many also settled in Washington, DC, Houston, and New York. The earthquakes, hurricanes, and mudslides that devastated El Salvador in the 1990s and 2000s prompted more people to flee their homeland. Most recently, the escalation of gang warfare in the 2010 decade has sent another wave of Salvadorans north to the United States.

In 2015, the number of El Salvador-born people living in the United States was about 1.17 million. Counting their US-born children, the number jumps to 2.1 million, making Salvadorans the largest Central American population in the country. They are also the second-largest unauthorized immigrant population in the Unites States, after Mexicans, since so many Salvadorans fled their country without visas. In general, these refugees have little formal

Salvadoran American parents and children attend storytime at a school in Washington, DC.

,education; therefore, many live in the United States illegally and work in temporary, low-paying jobs, such as babysitting, gardening, cleaning, and dog-walking. Most of these workers sent money to family back home. In 2012, The Salvadoran people in the United States transferred about $3.6 billion in remittances to El Salvador.

Few Salvadorans have been granted political asylum. Many US courts were reluctant to accept that Salvadorans were fleeing political violence rather than simply seeking out a better life, as this acknowledgment would have made it difficult for the United States to justify continuing its financial and military support of the war in El Salvador.

Even though many Salvadorans did not receive political asylum, a 1986 US amnesty law granted legal status to immigrants that entered the United States before 1982. In 1992 Salvadorans who had been in the United States since 1990 received a Temporary Protected Status (TPS), which allows them to live and work in the country. The TPS was offered again to Salvadorans following the 2001 earthquakes in El Salvador.

INTERNET LINKS

www.everyculture.com/multi/Pa-Sp/Salvadoran-Americans.html
This is a good narrative look at Salvadorans in the United States.

www.ipsnews.net/2012/05/native-people-of-el-salvador-finally-gain-recognition
This is a report on the recognition of indigenous people in the constitution.

www.minorityrights.org/4180/el-salvador/indigenous-peoples.html
This is a profile of the indigenous Nahua-Pipil people of El Salvador.

www.pewhispanic.org/2012/06/27/hispanics-of-salvadoran-origin-in-the-united-states-2010
This is a statistical overview of Salvadorans living in the United States.

LIFESTYLE

A Salvadoran girl faces many difficulties in her life ahead.

7

S ALVADORANS ARE A VERY SOCIABLE, hardworking, devout, and generous people, despite considerable hardship and adversity. Friends and family are central to daily life, although migration due to unemployment and civil war has broken apart many families and communities. Poverty abounds in El Salvador, and malnutrition is a serious problem, affecting one in every five children. Since most pregnant women are undernourished themselves, many children start life with serious nutritional deficiencies.

The lifestyle of the poor in El Salvador, whether in rural areas or in the cities, revolves around providing food and shelter for the family, and there is little time for leisure or education, or money for the modern conveniences that would make life easier and more pleasurable. Wealthier Salvadorans, on the other hand, own cars, work in office buildings, shop in malls, and live in modern houses.

RURAL LIFE

About half of all Salvadorans live in rural areas. The vast majority of them work for large landowners at an hourly wage that cannot pay for adequate food for their families. Houses are small and very basic,

Corrugated metal is often used in makeshift houses built by people in poverty.

transportation is generally by foot or by horse and cart, and long hours are spent getting through the day's work and household chores. At harvest time, the whole family works in the fields. Illiteracy is high, as children leave school at an early age to work or help out at home.

As most houses have no running water or electricity, rural Salvadorans use wood or charcoal to cook by fire, and burn candles or kerosene lamps for light. Water is usually collected from rivers and streams, even though the surface water is seriously polluted by agricultural and industrial waste. Because of the widespread danger of cholera, most people have developed the practice of disinfecting the water by adding bleach.

LIFE IN THE CITY

Almost a third of El Salvador's population lives in the capital city of San Salvador. The downtown streets are congested with cars, buses, street vendors, and pedestrians, and the air is thick with pollution. Most urban

Salvadorans work in factories, offices, and shops or as domestic workers. They shop at large central markets or modern, multistory shopping centers. The wide disparity between rich and poor is especially evident in San Salvador. The wealthy live in quiet, elegant suburbs, socialize in private clubs, dine in fine restaurants, and shop in expensive boutiques, while the poor live in slums on the edge of the city, getting by as best as they can.

A panoramic view of a slum in San Salvador shows many tin shacks.

HOUSING

RURAL The most common kind of house, the *choza* (CHO-sah), is made of woven branches and covered with mud. Others are made of adobe, or sun-dried mud bricks, which are sometimes whitewashed. Houses have dirt floors and thatched or tiled roofs, and few have running water or electricity. Living quarters are typically crowded, with six or more people living in one or two rooms that are divided by curtains rather than walls. Family members pull out cots, hammocks, or straw mats to sleep on at night.

THE WORKLOAD OF A RURAL WOMAN

A typical day for a rural woman begins before dawn. The first task is to fetch water, which may be as far as an hour's walk away. When she gets back, she gathers firewood, builds a fire, and makes the day's supply of tortillas. On top of buying food at the daily market, cooking, washing clothes in the river, cleaning the house, and caring for the children, her tasks include tending the garden and raising chickens and pigs. During the harvest season, she works on the farm alongside her husband, often without pay. She might also try to earn extra money for the family by selling vegetables, homemade fruit drinks, or candles in the local market or at a roadside stand.

URBAN The wealthy live in modern houses with swimming pools, well-tended gardens, and elaborate security systems. The small middle-class population lives in row houses or in comfortable apartments, either inside the city or in the suburbs. Most of the poor live in *tugurios* (tu-GU-ryos),

shantytowns made of tin or cardboard, with dirt floors, no electricity, and no access to running water or sewage services, while others rent rooms in crowded, rundown buildings called *mesones* (may-SON-ays)—chains of tiny, often windowless rooms surrounding a common courtyard, with a common latrine but no washing or cooking facilities.

Colorful, modest homes brighten the mountain village of Apaneca.

HEALTH CARE

The health of El Salvador's people has improved significantly since 1990. Maternal, neonatal, and under-five mortality rates have fallen. Life expectancy has risen. In 1985, the life expectancy for men was fifty-nine years and for women, sixty-eight years. A Salvadoran child born in 2015, on the other hand, could expect to live an average of seventy-four years—seventy-one years for men and nearly seventy-eight years for women.

Under the ARENA party presidential regimes, the government's health policy was moving toward the privatization of all medical services. By 2006, this approach had left 47 percent of Salvadorans outside of any health care system.

In 2009, with the election of the FMLN-backed president Mauricio Funes, the government of El Salvador launched a major health reform initiative. Its aim was universal health coverage. With that, the budget of the Ministry of Health was substantially increased.

The first thing government reformers did was to eliminate the "voluntary contributions" that patients had to make in order to receive hospital treatment. The payment wasn't voluntary at all, and those who could not pay for treatment were sent away. Even those hospital patients who could pay often had to bring their own food, bed sheets, soap, toilet paper, and even surgical supplies because hospitals were so poorly equipped. Once the "voluntary contributions" were eliminated, the number of births in hospitals increased by 30 percent between 2008 and 2012. In 2010, 92 percent of all births took place in hospitals.

The reformers also organized five hundred Community Health Teams to bring medical care to even the poorest regions of the country. Each team consists of a doctor, a nurse, and three health educators, and is responsible for about six hundred families.

At a neighborhood health center in San Salvador, a doctor talks to waiting patients.

Despite these improvements, serious health problems remain. Most are caused by poverty and include malnutrition, particularly of young children. Although chronic malnutrition among children under five has been declining since 1995, it still affects one out of every five youngsters. Violence is another factor that seriously affects children and adolescents. UNICEF, the United Nations Children's Fund, reports that in El Salvador, children under eighteen account for 12.8 percent of homicides, a statistical daily average of 1.5 deaths.

Family members walk down a street in Intipuca.

THE FAMILY

Traditionally the family is central to life in El Salvador, and families tend to be large, due partly to the dominance of Roman Catholicism, which is against contraception, and partly through necessity. In rural areas, especially, women are urged to marry young and have several children. Children are considered an economic asset. They are relied upon to help earn income for the family and to care for their parents in their old age.

Family unity is important, and extended families are common, with three generations often living under the same roof. Upper-class families are tied to one another by a complex web of marriage and kinship. This is one of the ways in which they have managed to hold on to their power and wealth.

Most births take place alone with the mother cutting the cord and burying the placenta, a Salvadoran tradition. Physician-assisted deliveries occur only in complicated pregnancies or emergency situations. The high birth rate is a way of compensating for the high infant mortality rate—many rural children die in their first year from disease or malnutrition.

The influence of Catholicism broadened the concept of family to include *padrinos* (pa-DREE-nos, or godfathers) and *madrinas* (ma-DREE-nas, or godmothers). Godparents played an important role in a child's upbringing.

Today, however, the practice of godparenting is less widespread. Family support has helped poor people endure the years of poverty and hardship, although civil war and chronic unemployment have taken their toll on family unity. Although Salvadoran society is traditionally patriarchal, as is the case in most of Latin America, many rural families are in fact headed by women, as the men left home in search of work or became casualties of the war. Common-law marriages and free unions are common in rural areas.

THE POSITION OF WOMEN

Women in El Salvador have faced widespread exploitation and oppression due to the circumstances of poverty, war, or simply tradition. Domestic abuse by fathers and husbands is common. Machismo, the Latin American ideal of manliness, dictates that men are superior to women, that a husband should earn the money for his family, and that the wife should do the "women's work" of cooking, cleaning, and caring for the children. The economic reality in

A girl participates in a march on International Day for the Elimination of Violence Against Women in San Salvador.

El Salvador, however, is that most families require two income-earning parents. The social reality is that many men abandon their wives, leaving approximately one-quarter of all Salvadoran households headed by women.

Guerrilla groups tried to overcome the widespread attitude of women as inferior beings. In the areas they controlled during the war, they discouraged wife-beating and stressed the equality of women in almost every aspect of work. Men and women shared responsibility for cooking, washing clothes, and working on construction and development projects.

Students work on laptops at a Catholic school in San Marcos.

Many Salvadoran women themselves have started to act as a force for positive change, forming organizations to tackle some of the fundamental issues that have prevented women from achieving equality, especially in rural areas. Such issues include the lack of education, high infant mortality rate, and high birth rate. These organizations provide a broad range of services, such as medical, legal, educational, childcare, family planning, and job placement.

The government has passed laws granting women equal legal status and "equal pay for equal work," but in practice many women still face discrimination in the workplace and are usually paid only half the salary that a man earns for the same work.

EDUCATION

The government provides free education up to grade nine (age fourteen), but only 82 percent of children make it that far. Many children, especially in the rural areas, do not attend school because the cost of supplies, transportation, school uniforms, and matriculation fees are too expensive for many poor families. This problem is compounded by a shortage of teachers and schools, and many children have to leave school after only a year or two in order to help support their family by working on plantations. At the secondary level, high rates of teen pregnancy and violence add to the difficulties of educating young people.

With the government committed to enforcing compulsory education, international agencies, such as World Bank and the United States Agency for International Development (USAID), have launched several programs to make education accessible to Salvadoran children in the rural areas.

TRANSPORTATION

El Salvador has more than 7,440 miles (12,000 km) of roads as well as two major highways (the Pan American Highway and the Carretora Litoral) that run the length of the country. These roads, however, are more likely to be traveled by buses and trucks than by private cars. A considerable number of roads were damaged by earthquakes in 2001, and the government began making repairs in the same year.

Taxis are plentiful in the capital city of San Salvador, but most Salvadorans get around by bus, bicycle, or on foot. In rural areas, horses are another

People nervously await a bus in San Salvador after gangs threatened violence against public transportation.

common form of transportation. The bus system is extensive and is the most popular method of traveling long distances.

Ferrocarriles Nacionales de El Salvador (FENADESAL), the national railway, is responsible for several hundred miles of railroad. The railway is used mainly for carrying goods and cargo, such as iron, cement, and dairy products. Like the roads, half of the railroad system was damaged by earthquakes in recent years, and El Salvador is working on the repairs.

The international airport near San Salvador is one of the most modern in the region and is served by a number of international airlines. Avianca El Salvador, the country's privately owned national airline, has a fleet of forty-four planes, and flies to fifty destinations in twenty-two countries.

SHOPPING

In San Salvador, the most popular shopping places are the central market and Metrocentro, a modern, split-level shopping mall offering a wide variety of goods in air-conditioned boutiques. Metrocentro is reputed to be the largest shopping mall in Central America. In smaller towns and villages, open-air markets and general stores stock a limited range of basic goods, such as clothing, food, and household items.

INTERNET LINKS

www.everyculture.com/Cr-Ga/El-Salvador.html
This site offers an overview of the Salvadoran lifestyle and culture.

www.kwintessential.co.uk/resources/global-etiquette/elsalvador.html
Here one can find advice for Salvadoran etiquette and customs, and a short explanation of machismo.

www.who.int/countryfocus/cooperation_strategy/ccsbrief_slv_en.pdf
This fact sheet from the World Health Organization offers an overview of the health situation in El Salvador.

RELIGION

The Monument to the Divine Savior of the World in
San Salvador depicts Jesus standing on the Earth.

8

ON SUNDAY, MARCH 23, 1980, IN THE early days of the El Salvadoran civil war, Óscar Romero, the Archbishop of San Salvador, delivered a sermon aimed at the government's soldiers:

"Brothers, you are a part of our own people. You are killing your own campesino brothers and sisters. Any human order to kill must be subordinate to the law of God, which says, 'Thou shalt not kill.' . . . In the name of God, in the name of this suffering people whose cries rise to heaven more loudly each day, I implore you, I beg you, I order you: Stop the repression."

Archbishop Oscar Romero smiles in 1979, about six months before he was killed.

The next day, while saying Mass in a hospital chapel, Archbishop Romero was assassinated.

That event, probably more than any other, demonstrated the cataclysmic collision of El Salvador's Roman Catholicism, history, and politics. Romero's funeral was the largest demonstration in Salvadoran history, perhaps even in the history of Latin America. Snipers, allegedly from the government, shot into the crowd, killing forty people and injuring many others.

Like much of Latin America, El Salvador is an intensely religious society—even non-practicing Catholics and people not affiliated with any religion say they pray at least once a day.

Roman Catholicism was brought to Latin America as part of the Spanish conquest, and it has played an extremely important role in shaping the culture of the region. In El Salvador, the Catholic Church generally supported the ruling classes and the social and economic systems that caused much hardship for the majority of Salvadorans. Even so, 83 percent of Salvadorans are Catholic. Church rituals and symbols have permeated society, and Catholicism's traditions of community, hierarchy, and social and family ties remain strong.

Membership in other religious denominations, including Baha'is, Evangelicals, Mormons, Seventh-Day Adventists, and Jehovah's Witnesses, is increasing, and gradually eroding the dominance of Roman Catholicism. Evangelical church services provide a supportive and charismatic environment that is particularly appealing to large numbers of Salvadorans who are poor and displaced from their community.

CATHOLICISM

The dominance of Catholicism in El Salvador is demonstrated by the number of religious holidays and festivals that fill the Salvadoran calendar and the abundance of Catholic churches, symbols, and shrines throughout the country. Every town and Catholic church in El Salvador has a patron saint, who is honored annually with great pomp and festivity.

The biggest patron saint event is held during the first week of August, in homage to El Salvador *del Mundo*, or "Savior of the World." Salvadorans

Catholic shrines in El Salvador attract pilgrims and visitors from far and wide. The Virgin Mary is a particularly important symbol, and several outdoor shrines have been erected in her honor.

An elegant white shrine, La Ceiba de Guadalupe, stands in San Salvador in tribute to the Virgin of Guadalupe. December 12 is her celebration day.

The small town of Cojutepeque near San Salvador attracts a steady flow of pilgrims, especially on May 13. There, in a large park on the Hill of the Turkeys, is a shrine to the Virgin of Fátima. The Virgin Mary is said to have appeared to three Portuguese shepherd children on May 13, 1917, in Fátima, Portugal. The statue was brought to El Salvador from Fátima in 1949.

celebrate by taking part in processions, fairs, carnival rides, and games. There are also lots of food and fireworks.

Despite its widespread popularity, Catholicism is beginning to lose its grip on many aspects of daily life. Both civil and religious marriage ceremonies are less prevalent in El Salvador than in other Latin American countries, and there is a relatively high rate of family breakdown. Divorces and common-law marriages are on the rise, and many children are born out of wedlock. Also, the practice of selecting godparents for children is becoming less widespread.

ABORTION El Salvador amended its constitution in 1999 to recognize that life begins at the moment of conception. This effectively bans abortions on

Even though Catholicism in El Salvador is waning, the people still observe some formalities associated with the religion. For example, public holidays in El Salvador center on religious events, such as Christmas and Easter, and every town has a festival for its patron saint.

An elderly Catholic woman attends Mass on Ash Wednesday.

In the past, Salvadorans attached a lot of importance to the rites of passage. They christened and baptized their babies into the church. Padrinos, or godparents, were carefully chosen for each child and were given the responsibility of guiding the child's spiritual— and sometimes material— development. Entrance into adulthood during the child's fifteenth year was celebrated with a church ceremony called a quinciñera *(keen-see-NYE-rah). Weddings were always formal occasions and usually took place in a church, and death was observed with a* vela *(VAY-lah), or wake.*

Today, however, not all of these are commonly practiced by Salvadorans. Social and economic conditions have changed, particularly during and after the civil war.

any grounds. Critics say that the timing, just before elections, was to garner the votes of Catholics, who form the majority of the population. Human rights advocates say the ban endangers the lives of young girls who get pregnant, often as the result of force or ignorance, and adds to the growing problem of teen motherhood.

LIBERATION THEOLOGY

In the late 1960s some members of the Roman Catholic Church in El Salvador were inspired by the Second Vatican Council's reforms on Catholicism and the Second Latin American Bishops' Conference's resolution on greater efforts to help the poor. They began saying Mass in Spanish instead of Latin and applying the Bible to contemporary problems. Priests and lay leaders began to work with the poor and tried to improve their quality of life physically as well as spiritually. People formed small groups called Christian Base Communities (CEB), which discussed how situations described in the Bible could be applied to their own lives, and started agitating for change.

In San Salvador, a woman marches on International Day of Action for the Decriminalization of Abortion in 2012.

As a result of this challenge to the existing social and political order, many members of the oligarchy and the military began to view the Church as subversive and Communist. Several church workers and members of CEBs became targets of violence. The Vatican viewed it as too political.

Violence continued throughout the 1980s, causing so many priests to resign that nearly half of the rural parishes were left without one. Many of the CEBs dissolved or went underground, continuing their activities in secret. Many lay leaders of the CEBs joined the guerrillas, and some priests continued working in the conflict zones, trying to emphasize the need for social and political organization among the poor. Many were assassinated. The death of Archbishop Romero and other popular priests turned them into martyrs and added fire to the cause.

Faced with the rise of liberation theology and a challenge to the status quo, in 1977 the Vatican appointed Óscar Arnulfo Romero to be the new archbishop and to reinforce a conservative authority in El Salvador.

As Romero became familiar with the reality of life in El Salvador, however, he began to speak out against the widespread repression and poverty he saw. He encouraged workers to campaign for an increase in wages and a redistribution of land, and he called on the government to end repression and bring about social justice.

Within two years the small, soft-spoken, and bespectacled Romero had become a much-loved figure among the ordinary people of El Salvador. But he was viewed as a major threat by the government and the military. Branded as a guerrilla, he was assassinated while celebrating Mass on March 24, 1980. The murder shocked people both inside and outside El Salvador and was one of the events that sparked the outbreak of civil war. Ironically, Pope John Paul II had decided to remove Romero from the post of Archbishop of San Salvador. He had just signed the removal order on the morning of March 24.

Although the government officially attributed the murder to unidentified members of right wing death squads, Roberto d'Aubuisson, leader of the ARENA party, was widely believed to be responsible. At the end of the civil war twelve years later, the Truth Commission, mandated by the peace agreement to investigate the worst crimes of the war, found that d'Aubuisson had indeed ordered the murder of Archbishop Romero, and likely thousands of others. However, d'Aubuisson had died the year before of cancer and no one else has ever been prosecuted for the crime.

Although many in El Salvador already refer to the archbishop as "San Romero" and have proclaimed him the unofficial patron saint of the country, he isn't actually a saint—at least not yet. However, he does appear to be headed in that direction. In 2015, Romero was beatified by Pope Francis. In Roman Catholicism, beatification is the last step on the canonization path before sainthood.

PROTESTANTS

Protestantism has enjoyed tremendous growth and has contributed to the decline of the Catholic Church in El Salvador. Evangelical missionaries, primarily from the United States, have become so influential that all non-Catholic groups working and preaching in Central America, including Presbyterians, Lutherans, Mormons, and Jehovah's Witnesses, are referred to as evangelicals.

Although evangelicals use some of the same techniques as liberation theologists, meeting in small groups and emphasizing prayer and personal responsibility, they generally discourage efforts to achieve social and political change and have thus won the support of the oligarchy and the military. On the other hand, some of the more mainstream Protestant groups, such as Baptists, Episcopalians, and Lutherans, espoused liberation theology and won many converts among the poor.

NATIVE RELIGION

The religion practiced by indigenous people in Central America has been described by anthropologists as Christo-pagan due to its complex mix of indigenous beliefs and the Christianity of early Roman Catholic missionaries.

Christian baptism, for example, is the first major event in the life of an individual, and a child is not considered fully human until the baptism has been performed. At the other end of the life cycle, the usual Christian rituals are observed. At funerals, the body is buried, church bells are rung, incense is burned, and prayers are read in church and at the graveside. Christian deities and saints have replaced the hierarchy of indigenous supernatural beings, but pagan beliefs remain. For example, disease is attributed to witchcraft or the failure to appease evil spirits.

FOLK BELIEFS

Belief in the power of witchcraft and the devil is widespread, and good and evil spirits are prominent figures in folktales. *Brujería* (brew-hay-REE-ya),

Archbishop Romero made a radical shift away from conservatism after the assassination of his good friend Father Rutilio Grande. Father Rutilio was a Jesuit priest who believed in liberation theology and was outspoken in defense of the poor. When Father Rutilio was killed, Archbishop Romero felt he could no longer ignore the brutality of the government.

THE AZTEC STORY OF CREATION

Indigenous people in Central America believed that four worlds, or Suns, were created by gods and then destroyed by catastrophes before the present universe came into being.

According to the Aztec legend of creation, the first Sun was called Four-Jaguar and was destroyed by jaguars. At the end of the second Sun, Four-Wind, mankind was transformed into monkeys by a hurricane unleashed by the wind god. The god of thunder and lightning put an end to the third Sun, Four-Rain, with a rain of fire. The fourth Sun, Four-Water, ended in a massive flood that lasted for fifty-two years. The fifth and present Sun, Four-Earthquake, was created by the rain god and is doomed to be destroyed by a tremendous earthquake.

The Aztecs believed that their mission was to prevent the fifth destruction of the Earth, and that the only way of doing this was to give offerings and make sacrifices.

This carved Aztec relief depicts the sun god and four epochs of the creation and destruction of the universe.

or witchcraft, is really a form of native medicine practiced in some rural areas. The *curandero* (cur-ahn-DE-roh), or witch doctor, is believed to have special healing powers and uses herbs and other traditional medicines to treat illnesses that do not respond to conventional Western medicine. For example, people from the city travel to villages to ask a *curandero* for special powders and rituals that they hope will improve their love life.

A traditional remedy for a sick baby involves the *curandero* rubbing garlic paste on the baby's body, hanging a ring of garlic around the baby's neck, praying, and holding an egg up to the sun; if the *curandero* can see a small circle in the white part of the egg, it means that someone has looked at the baby with "sight that is too strong," and the treatment of garlic paste and prayer is continued.

INTERNET LINKS

www.nytimes.com/2015/05/23/world/americas/honor-comes-late-tooscar-romero-a-martyr-for-the-poor.html?ref=topics
Romero's beatification was an emotional occasion for Salvadorans.

www.osv.com/OSVNewsweekly/Article/TabId/535/ArtMID/13567/ArticleID/17106/The-martyrdom-of-Archbishop-Oscar-Romero.aspx
This site offers a very good look at the life and death of Romero on the thirty-fifth anniversary of his assassination.

www.photius.com/countries/el_salvador/society/el_salvador_society_the_role_of_religion.html
This very interesting article from 1988 traces the roles of the Catholic Church, liberation theology, and Evangelical Protestantism in El Salvador.

www.washingtonpost.com/news/acts-of-faith/wp/2015/04/08/christianity-is-growing-rapidly-in-el-salvador-along-with-gang-violence-and-murder-rates
Here, find an interesting look at religion and gang violence in El Salvador today.

LANGUAGE

ALTO

Traffic signs are written in Spanish.

9

SPANISH IS THE OFFICIAL LANGUAGE of El Salvador and is spoken by the vast majority of its citizens. Historically, it has been normal for the language of the colonizer, or the conqueror, to become the language of the land. In the past, however, there was no regard or respect for the language or customs of the native peoples. The thought then was that the sooner the natives adapted to the ways of the "superior" colonial culture, the better. If native languages died, then better yet. Those languages would only prevent the people from acclimating.

Today's thinking is different. Just as with animals, extinct is forever. A dead language—especially one that had no written form—is usually impossible to bring back to life. Languages are precious records of how a culture thought, expressed itself, and what it valued.

While native languages have continued to flourish in some Central and South American countries—Mayan in Guatemala, Quechua in Peru, and Guaraní in Paraguay, for example—the indigenous languages of El Salvador have died out in daily use. Nahua and Lenca, derived

The local Spanish vernacular, or everyday tongue, is called *Caliche* (ka-lee-chay). It incorporates words from the indigenous Nahuatl, and is often used in rural areas and with children.

from the Nahuatl language of the Aztecs, began to decline when Spain colonized El Salvador in the sixteenth century and most indigenous people became assimilated into Spanish-American culture. The massacre of thirty thousand native people in 1932 further eroded the use of indigenous languages. At that time, most of the country's remaining native people were forced to abandon their languages, customs, and costumes in order to survive.

On August 25, 2015, a man reads a newspaper with the headline "Terrorists," in reference to the Constitutional Court declaring gangs to be terrorist groups.

INDIGENOUS LANGUAGES

Chilanga, a Lencan language, is now extinct in El Salvador. In the 1970s, researchers identified only one Lencan speaker remaining in Chilanga, El Salvador. Indigenous groups are trying to revive the language, but it might be too late. Pipil, a Nahua language, is close to extinction as well. It has already disappeared in Guatemala, Honduras, and Panama. Pipil, called Nawat by the native people, is spoken mostly by a few elderly speakers in the Salvadoran departments of Sonsonate and Ahuachapán in the western part of the country. It's too soon to say if recent efforts to teach the language to the next generation will succeed.

The most obvious legacy of these languages exists in the country's geographical names. *Cuscatlán*, the Nahua name for the area that includes present-day El Salvador, means "Land of the Jewel." Towns and villages such as Chalchuapa, Nahuizalco, and Zacatecoluca all bear names of Pipil origin. Many of the natural landmarks also retain their indigenous names, such as the Izalco Volcano, the Lempa River, and Lake Coatepeque. Most of the volcanoes have both an indigenous name and a Spanish name: the San Salvador Volcano, for instance, is also known as Quetzaltepec, meaning "mountain of quetzal birds" in Nahua.

In the tenth century, at the height of the Arabic civilization in Asia and Europe, the survival of Spanish in the world seemed unlikely. A few hundred years later, however, Spanish had become a major colonizing language, and today, Spanish is spoken by twelve times as many people outside than inside Spain.

Spanish gained its first foothold in the Americas when the explorer Hernán Cortés landed in 1519 and overthrew Montezuma's Aztec Empire. As the Spanish conquistadores spread across the continent in search of gold, they brought their language with them.

Spanish is now the official language of all mainland countries in Central and South America, with the exception of Brazil, Belize, and the Guyanas. From Mexico to the tip of Argentina, Spanish is spoken by more than 360 million people.

Hernan Cortés meets the Aztec Emperor Montezuma.

SPANISH

The Spanish spoken in El Salvador and other Central and South American countries is close to that of Spain, although there are some variations in local vocabulary and expressions. A soft drink, for example, is called a *gaseosa* (ga-say-OH-sah) in El Salvador and Honduras, a soda (SOH-dah) in Panama, and a *fresco* (FRAY-skoh) in Nicaragua. One feature common to the pronunciation in all of Spanish America is the tendency to make s, z, and soft c into the same sound s.

SALVADORAN PRONUNCIATION

Unlike Spanish speakers in some Latin American countries, Salvadorans typically speak clearly and precisely, pronouncing every syllable of every word. Here are some examples:

a. . . . . *a as in cart*

e. . . . . *e as in they or a as in day*

i. . . . . *ee as in meet*

o. . . . . . . *o as in note*

u. . . . . . . *oo as in toot or u as in flute*

y. . . . . . . *ee as in meet or y as in yet*

b. . . . . *b as in boy*

c. . . . . *s as in sit when before e or i, or k as in kind*

ch . . . . *ch as in child*

d. . . . . *d as in dog; or resembles th as in they when at the end of a word*

f. . . . . . . *f as in off*

g. . . . . *g as in go, or, when before e or i, a guttural ch as in loch*

h. . . . . . . *silent*

j. . . . . *h as in hat*

l. . . . . *l as in ball*

ll. . . . . *y as in yet*

m . . . . *m as in map*

n. . . . . *n as in noon*

ñ. . . . . *ny as in canyon*

p. . . . . *p as in purse*

q. . . . . . . *k as in kind*

r. . . . . *rolled, especially when at the beginning of a word*

rr . . . . *strongly rolled*

s . . . . *s as in sit*

t. . . . . *t as in tilt*

v. . . . . *b as in boy*

x. . . . . *x as in exit*

z. . . . . *s as in sit*

Although Spanish has replaced the indigenous languages in El Salvador, it has also been influenced by them. When the colonists came across new types of food and animals, they used an approximation of the native names to create new words: thus *maíz* (may-EES, corn), *cacao* (ka-KAH-oh, cocoa), and *ananás* (ah-nah-NAHS, pineapple), as well as tapir, jaguar, and llama.

NAMES AND TITLES

Many Salvadorans follow the Spanish custom of having two or more surnames, taking the patrimonial surname from both parents to form the surname. For instance, Liliana Guadalupe Escobar Hernández officially has four names: the first two are hers alone; the third name, Escobar, is her father's surname, which was also his father's family name; the fourth name, Hernández, is her mother's family name. Formally, Liliana is known as Señorita Escobar Hernández, often shortened to Señorita Escobar. If she marries a man named Oscar Hurtado Gómez, she will take the patrilineal part of his surname and add it to hers: Liliana Guadalupe Escobar Hurtado. Then she will formally be called Señora Hurtado.

DIGITAL COMMUNICATIONS

There are some 1.7 million Internet users in El Salvador, about 27 percent of the population. Cybercafes are common in the cities and most hotels offer free Wi-Fi access. As of September 2012, the country had 1,491,480 Facebook users. There are about a dozen El Salvadoran newspapers online, all in Spanish. Cell phones are virtually universal in most populated areas.

INTERNET LINKS

pazamorelsalvador.wordpress.com/language-and-phrases
Some words of Salvadoran Caliche Spanish are noted here.

www.veintemundos.com/en/spanish/el-salvador
This is a quick look at languages in El Salvador, with some local phrases.

ARTS

A man sits by a mural of Archbishop Oscar Romero in Ciudad Barrios, where Romero was born.

10

G IVEN EL SALVADOR'S TURBULENT past, it's not surprising that much of the country's artistic expression has been influenced by politics. Paintings, plays, books, and music typically contain elements that are political in nature. At least three of the best-known Salvadoran writers have been forced to flee government repression for their political activities, and they live in exile abroad.

Manlio Argueta's novel *One Day of Life* (1980) was once banned by the government of El Salvador for its descriptions of atrocities by the Organización Democrática Nacionalista or ORDEN, the government's paramilitary intelligence organization. The novel is considered one of the best Latin American books of the twentieth century.

A visitor takes in an art exhibition at the Museum of Art in San Salvador.

These three pre-Columbian warriors date to around 600 CE.

El Salvador also has a strong tradition of popular art in the form of folk music, popular theater, and folk art. Elements of indigenous art have begun to influence Salvadoran music and painting.

ANCIENT ARTS AND CRAFTS

Most of what is known of Mayan and Aztec art forms is drawn from archaeological discoveries of ancient artifacts. Musical instruments, pottery vessels, stone sculptures, and jewelry made from copper, gold, and jade attest to the magnificence of the crafts produced by native people thousands of years ago. Many of the artifacts unearthed during archaeological expeditions at the ruins of ancient cities in El Salvador are now housed in the Museo Nacional Davíd J. Guzmán—the national museum in San Salvador—and at the Tazumal Museum.

Musical instruments include pipes with as many as six finger holes; drums, called *huehuetls* (hway-HWAY-tls), made from wood or clay and originally covered with deerskin; marimbas, or wooden xylophones, which were introduced to the Pipil from Mexico and Guatemala; the *pito* (PEE-toh),

THE MURAL ON THE CATHEDRAL

In 1997, five years after the peace accords, artist Fernando Llort created a ceramic mural for the façade of the Metropolitan Cathedral in San Salvador. The mural, done in Llort's abstract folkloric style, pictured colorful peasants, horses, crops, and birds of peace, along with traditional indigenous and Christian imagery. Titled "Harmony of My People," it was a celebration of peace.

In December 2011, a large white sheet covered the mural as workers chipped off all 2,700 pieces of mural tile. The Archbishop of San Salvador, Jose Luis Escobar Alas, had ordered the removal of the mural without consulting the national government or the artist.

People were outraged. Llort is the country's most popular and important living artist, and his work is seen as expressing El Salvador's cultural identity. The cathedral itself, originally constructed in 1842, serves much the same purpose. It has been destroyed many times by earthquakes and fires, but always rebuilt, most recently completed in 1999. It was the site of the historic funeral of Archbishop Óscar Romero and holds his remains.

The nation's Secretary of Culture formally condemned the act. He declared it against El Salvador's cultural patrimony law, which states that changes to historical and cultural monuments in need of restoration must be approved by his office. The archbishop, meanwhile, offered little in the way of explanation, and in the end, nothing happened.

Men play instruments during a religious procession in the town of Tepecoyo.

a high-pitched whistle that sounds like a flute; and the *chirmía* (cheer-MEE-ah), which is a pipe with a reed mouthpiece that sounds rather like a clarinet. Percussion instruments include the *tambor* (tam-BOHR), a large drum played with one hand on each side, and the *tun* (TOON), a small box drum.

PAINTING

It was not until the twentieth century that El Salvador produced notable painters. The most famous Salvadoran painter is José Mejía Vides, who is sometimes called the "Painter of Panchimalco" because he often portrays small-town life in his paintings. His vivid, simple style shows the influence of Mexico's famous muralists and of the French painter Paul Gauguin.

Julia Díaz (1917—1999) is El Salvador's best-known female painter. She studied in Paris, and her work has been exhibited in the United States, Europe, and Latin America. Other prominent Salvadoran painters include Raúl Elas Reyes, Luis Ángel Salinas, Camilio Minero, and Noé Canjura.

A notable and unique school of art has been founded by Salvadoran painter Fernando Llort (b. 1949) in La Palma, a town in the mountains north of San Salvador. La Palma art uses bright colors and a naive style to portray religious themes, as well as the peasants, the farm animals, and the red-roofed white adobe houses of rural El Salvador. The images are painted onto various items, such as wooden crosses, towels, or chests of drawers, cast into ceramics, or finely etched on seeds to be worn as pendants. Llort has also produced many excellent sculptures and canvas paintings, which he displays in his own gallery, El Árbol de Dios, in San Salvador. In 2013, he was awarded the country's National Prize of Culture.

The bold, distinctive style of Fernando Llort is unmistakable in this detail from one of his paintings.

HANDICRAFTS

Since the time of the Maya many thousands of years ago, crafts have played a prominent role among the people of Central America. Musical instruments, pottery vessels, stone sculptures, architectural ornaments, and jewelry found

at the sites of ruined cities offer proof of the level of skill attained by Mayan craftsmen. In some areas, entire communities specialized in a particular craft. Craftsmen were organized into guilds and enjoyed considerable prestige in society.

Several native villages near San Salvador continue to specialize in traditional handicrafts. Ilobasco, one of the country's foremost traditional craft villages, is famous for its intricate ceramics and *sorpresas* (sorh-PRAY-sas), or surprises, which are tiny clay figures and nativity scenes hidden inside walnut-sized oval shells.

A man selling colorful handmade hammocks waits for customers in downtown San Salvador.

Basketry is the specialty of Nahuizalco, a Pipil village. Colorful hammocks and other woven textiles made on handmade wooden looms form the basis of San Sebastián's economy.

LITERATURE

Poetry has a strong tradition in El Salvador and is extremely popular among people from all walks of life. The nineteenth century poet Juan José Cañas Gavidia spent most of his life living abroad and writing nostalgically about El Salvador's lakes and volcanoes.

Poet, essayist, playwright, translator, historian, and dramatist Francisco Antonio Gavidia died in 1955 at the age of ninety-two. His most important poem, *To Central America*, condemned tyranny and expressed faith in democracy and the unity of Central America.

Salvador Salazar Arrué, who wrote under the pen name Salarrué, was a novelist, short story writer, and painter. His short story, *Cuentos de*

Barro, or *Tales of Mud*, is said to mark the beginning of the modern Central American short story genre.

Two of the best and most controversial writers of the twentieth century are Roque Dalton and Manlio Argueta. Dalton was a poet and historian who was born into a wealthy family but spoke out against El Salvador's social injustices. He was arrested by government forces and sentenced to be executed, but he escaped and went into exile from 1960 to 1973. When he returned to El Salvador, he joined the guerrilla army but was charged with spying. He was tried and executed by the guerrillas in 1975. *Clandestine Poems*, the collection of poetry that he wrote when he returned secretly to El Salvador for a short while in 1965, was translated into English in 1984.

A book vendor piles up his wares at an outdoor stall.

Argueta writes about the daily life and struggles of the Salvadoran peasants. He was expelled from El Salvador because of his political activism and lived in exile in Costa Rica until the end of the civil war in El Salvador. His books, *One Day of Life* and *Cuzcatlán*, have been translated into English.

MUSIC

Formal music performances are held at San Salvador's National Theater. David Granadino and Felipe Soto are two renowned nineteenth century composers whose music is still performed today. One of El Salvador's most famous twentieth century composers is María Mendoza de Baratta, who is greatly influenced by indigenous Salvadoran music.

Men play folk music in a park in San Salvador.

Canción popular (kan-see-OHN poh-poo-LAHR), or folk music, which describes daily life and current events in El Salvador, is performed in bars, cafés, at music festivals, and at an open forum called a *peña* (PAY-nya), where anyone from the audience can stand up and play or sing. Andean folk music, the distinctive Incan music of the Andes played on pan pipes and flutes, is also popular in El Salvador.

In the 1990s, hip hop and reggaeton found an audience with Salvadoran young people. Groups such as Pescozada expressed opinions about the country's problems.

THEATER

Formal theatrical performances are held at the ornate National Theater in San Salvador. Contemporary dramatists include Waldo Chávez Velasco, who writes fantasy, and Italo López Vallecillos and Alvaro Menén Desleal, both distinguished popular authors of political and philosophical works.

Popular theater, on the other hand, is usually performed in cafés and at outdoor festivals, and often draws from political subject matter. During the civil war, this type of theater was often performed with a certain degree of risk, because it usually carried a message of protest against the government, and the military often responded with harassment and violence against the performers.

The National Theater is one of the capital city's most notable buildings.

INTERNET LINKS

www.fernando-llort.com/biography
Here find a biography of Fernando Llort, one of El Salvador's leading contemporary artists.

hyperallergic.com/114155/creating-a-national-art-in-el-salvador
A tour of the Museum of Art in El Salvador (MARTE) offers an overview of the growth of a national art.

thelatinoauthor.com/countries/literature/literature-el-salvador
A nice overview of Salvadoran literature is found here.

www.lehman.cuny.edu/ciberletras/v08/arias.html
Here is an insightful interview with author Manlio Argueta.

publicwalls.org/2014/07/15/feature-el-salvadors-president-opens-official-residence-as-an-art-gallery
This has some beautiful examples of Salvadoran painting.

LEISURE

A young man takes a daring dive off a waterfall.

11

LIKE MANY LATIN AMERICAN countries, El Salvador is a nation of soccer fans. The game is extremely popular, both to watch and to play. Those who cannot afford to buy a proper soccer ball make do with a nylon stocking wrapped around a ball of rags.

In 2013, the Salvadoran national soccer team suffered a bruising scandal. Several players were accused of purposely losing matches in exchange for money in games against Venezuela, Mexico, the United States, and Costa Rica. After an investigation, fourteen players were handed immediate lifetime bans from the game. Others received temporary bans.

Two brothers play soccer with their uncle in a parking lot.

Politics can intrude into the realm of sports, as it did in the Soccer War (or Football War) of 1969. At the time, approximately three hundred thousand Salvadorans were living illegally in Honduras, refugees from the poverty and repression in overcrowded El Salvador. Resentment among Hondurans against the Salvadoran squatters had been growing, and Honduras passed a land reform law taking land occupied by Salvadoran immigrants and giving it to native-born Hondurans. Salvadorans were expelled from Honduras by the thousands. Hostilities rose to a fevered pitch in a series of soccer games played between the two countries as part of a World Cup preliminary in June 1969.

Fighting erupted between fans on both sides at the first game in Tegucigalpa, the capital of Honduras. Violence escalated at the second game in San Salvador. There, Salvadoran fans harassed Honduran team members and fans and insulted the Honduran flag and national anthem. Salvadorans still in Honduras suffered from retaliatory acts by Hondurans. The third game took place in Mexico City, with a win for El Salvador. As soon as it ended, El Salvador cut all diplomatic ties with Honduras.

Within two weeks, El Salvador launched a military strike against Honduras. The Organization of American States (OAS) promptly got involved and arranged a cease-fire. Although the war was brief, more than two thousand lives were lost, and the actual peace settlement took more than ten years to achieve. Some parts of the dispute—mainly land disputes—remain active even today.

Honduran Air Force pilots convene just before the start of the Football War in 1969.

Daily life is hard work in El Salvador, especially in rural areas. With the whole family toiling long hours just to get by, there is little time left for play and little or no money for toys or hobbies. Salvadoran children still play when they can, of course, making toys from sticks, tin cans, stones, or rags, and playing *mica* (MEE-ka), or tag.

After the evening meal, friends and neighbors often gather together. Wealthier Salvadorans living in the capital have more sophisticated leisure choices: they can dine in fine restaurants, see plays at the National Theater, dance in night clubs, or listen to concerts performed by El Salvador's symphony orchestra.

A child plays in polluted Ilopango Lake.

STORYTELLING

A more common form of entertainment is storytelling. It does not cost anything, does not require any electrical gadgets or a knowledge of reading, and it can be used by mothers to entertain their children while carrying out household tasks. The same stories are heard all over the country, although

DEVILISH FOLKTALES

The devil is a central figure in Salvadoran folktales. People try to avoid him out of fear that he will tempt them into giving their souls to him. One well-known story is Justo Juez de la Noche, *or* Just Judge of the Night. *The Just Judge is a tall man wearing a black suit who appears only at midnight. No one has ever seen his face, but his eyes are "like fire." He usually appears before lone travelers, especially in rural areas.*

In one version of the story, a man named Julio is walking alone one night when he sees a very tall man blocking his path. The tall man, of course, is the Just Judge, although Julio does not know it. They walk and talk together for a long time. Suddenly, the Just Judge whips out his machete and tries to strike Julio with it, but Julio is experienced with a machete. He manages to strike the Just Judge with his own machete, but the blow has no effect. Instead, the Just Judge simply laughs with a roar so loud that it can be heard from miles away. Julio sees the red eyes for the first time, and he runs away to avoid losing his soul, but he cannot escape losing his mind.

they often have regional variations; common themes include the devil, who is typically disguised, and the struggle between good and evil. Among native groups, ancient legends about the creation of the world and of human beings are an important part of the culture, as well as a form of entertainment.

TELEVISION AND RADIO

In a small town on a Saturday night, it is not uncommon to see half the townspeople crowded around the doorway of a single small house lit by the bluish glow of a television—especially if a soccer match is on. Although El Salvador has several television stations, television sets are scarce, due to the widespread poverty and shortage of electricity. There are only about two hundred televisions for

A woman jokes with a reveler dressed as the devil during the opening parade of the Savior of the World festivities.

American television programs, food brands, fashion trends, and leisure activities have made their presence felt throughout much of the world, and El Salvador is no exception.

Baseball and skate-boarding are popular pastimes. Fast-food restaurants, such as McDonald's, Pizza Hut, and Dunkin' Donuts, are easily found in the capital city of San Salvador and are much frequented by the young. Coca-Cola and Pepsi are the best-known brands of soft drinks, and jeans are worn by men and women in El Salvador from all walks of life.

American situation comedies and series dominate the country's television channels, providing young Salvadorans with examples of the latest hairstyles, clothing, and verbal expressions. Pop songs from popular American music bands can be heard on many of El Salvador's radio stations.

every thousand people, and in rural areas television is almost non-existent. Those who do have a set sometimes offset the cost by charging their neighbors a few cents to watch it. Radios are more prevalent, and El Salvador has more than two hundred radio stations. Unlike its larger neighbors, El Salvador does not produce any of its own movies or television programs; most of them are imported from the United States or Mexico and are either dubbed into Spanish or given Spanish subtitles. Only city dwellers have access to movie theaters.

MUSIC AND DANCING

Salvadorans love getting together to sing, play music, and dance. The songs are often religious in nature, especially in church communities, or they tell a story. Rock music from abroad is popular among young people and is played in nightclubs and discos in San Salvador, but everyone enjoys dancing to Latino music, such as the lively *cumbia* (coom-BEE-ah) and salsa or the romantic *ranchera* (rahn-CHEH-ra).

A happy couple dances during the Senior Citizen Festival in San Salvador.

Small towns and villages in El Salvador, as in much of Latin America, are built around a central square, or plaza, which serves as the hub of the town's social, economic, and political life. The most important buildings, such as the church, the town hall, and the main stores border the plaza. The square is usually planted with trees, flowers, and shrubs, and is a popular center for playing games, relaxing, and socializing.

SPORTS

Volleyball, basketball, baseball, and softball are popular in El Salvador, but soccer, called *fútbol* ("football"), is the country's national sport. Its fans are passionate in their enjoyment of the game, whether they are playing it themselves or just watching it. Almost every city has a soccer stadium, and young boys join neighborhood or school teams at an early age, hoping to be chosen one day to play for the Selección Nacional, the national team.

WATER SPORTS Popular in El Salvador, especially during the hottest months, are water sports. Wealthier Salvadorans enjoy swimming at private clubs or beaches, water-skiing, boating, and fishing, while poor rural children are happy simply to splash about in lakes or rivers while their mothers wash clothes. One of the most popular spots for swimming is Los Chorros, a beautiful park near San Salvador.

A surfer performs an aerial stunt at a famous surfing spot on Punta Roca beach.

INTERNET LINKS

www.americasquarterly.org/node/3027
This list of things to do in El Salvador is aimed at tourists, but gives an idea of Salvadoran life.

www.espnfc.us/team/el-salvador/2650/index
ESPN has English-language coverage of El Salvador sports.

www.laprensagrafica.com/Futbol-Nacional-LMF
This online newspaper covers Salvadoran national fútbol, but is only available in Spanish.

sansalvador.usembassy.gov/news/2014/07/23.html
This is a description of a USAID youth outreach program for the prevention of youth violence.

FESTIVALS

Children participate in the annual Panchimalco Flower and Palm Festival in 2015.

12

P ARADES, FIREWORKS, MUSIC, and plenty of good food—this is how Salvadorans celebrate their Independence Day, September 15. In fact, it's how they celebrate quite a few festive occasions.

Most of the major holidays are religious and are the cause of particularly lengthy revelry—Christmas and Easter celebrations each last a full week. In addition, each city, village, and town has an annual festival for its patron saint, and some small towns embellish their town festivals with rich indigenous traditions.

Cadets of the Salvadoran Army demonstrate their skills at a ceremony.

On May 3, the Day of the Cross, people place a cross in their yards, and decorate it with fruit and garlands. Tradition has it that the cross will prevent the devil from dancing at their doors. The faithful then go from house to house to kneel and make the sign of the cross before their neighbor's displays.

New Year's Eve . . . . *December 31*

New Year's Day . . . . *January 1*

Palm Sunday . . . . *March/April (variable)*

Easter Sunday . . . . *March/April (variable)*

Labor Day . . . . *May 1*

Day of the Virgin of Fátima . . . . *May 13*

Festival of El Salvador del Mundo . . . . *August 3–6*

Independence Day . . . . *September 15*

Columbus Day . . . . *October 12*

All Souls' Day . . . . *November 2*

Anniversary of First Call for Independence . . . . *November 5*

Day of the Virgin of Guadalupe . . . . *December 12*

Christmas . . . . *December 25–31*

SEMANA SANTA

Holy Week, or Semana Santa, begins the week before Easter with Palm Sunday and is cause for grand celebrations within the Catholic Church. Catholics celebrate Palm Sunday, the day representing Jesus' entry into Jerusalem, by walking to Mass bearing flowers and palm branches. In some towns the streets are carpeted with flowers and lined with pictures of the Virgin Mary and Jesus.

All the stages of Christ's crucifixion and ascent into heaven are played out through dramatic ritual and elaborate celebration. The Last Supper is observed at Mass when the priest washes the feet of twelve men, just as the Bible says that Jesus washed the feet of his twelve disciples. On the Thursday, Friday, or Saturday of Semana Santa, they symbolically mourn the death of Jesus by giving up some personal comfort or luxury.

On Good Friday, a group of people carry a cross and a life-size image of Jesus through town, while singing songs of his suffering. When the procession

arrives at the church, it is met by more people carrying an image of Jesus nailed to the cross. In the town of Izalco, the image of Jesus on the cross is so large that it takes seventy-five people to carry it. The image of Jesus is taken down from the cross at three o'clock in the afternoon. People wrap the image in white sheets and keep a candlelight vigil at the church throughout the night.

The tone of the entire day is very serious. Children are not supposed to run, because Judas ran after he betrayed Christ. Indeed, children generally do not play on Good Friday, nor do people travel, out of respect for Jesus' torturous journey to Calvary. Semana Santa is sincerely celebrated in El Salvador because so many people feel that it is symbolic of their own suffering and their hope for renewed life.

On Easter Saturday, people spend the day relaxing. They might sleep in late, then pack a lunch of tamales, watermelon, tortillas, and beans before spending the afternoon at the ocean or the nearest river. In the evening, they attend Mass. Outside the church, they circle around a bonfire; the priest uses

Catholics carry statues of Jesus in a Holy Week procession in Izalco.

A procession for Semana Santa features an elaborate casket.

the flames to light a candle, which in turn is used to light all the parishioners' candles. Then they enter the church in a lighted procession, which is meant to symbolize Christ before his resurrection from the dead.

The somber tone of Semana Santa ends on Easter Sunday, which is known as Pascua. People joyously celebrate by marching in a procession, again carrying the image of Jesus. They receive a blessing from the priest with holy water, and some people bring their animals to be blessed as well.

Semana Santa is especially beautiful in the smaller towns, where people celebrate the holiday to the fullest.

CHRISTMAS

The season of Christmas begins a full month before Christmas Day, and continues into January. As with Semana Santa, it is especially celebrated in the Catholic Church. Beginning on November 26, church members practice *posadas* (po-SAH-das), or inns, taking statues of the Virgin Mary and Joseph from house to house every night until December 23, and spending a few hours singing, eating, and praying together at each house.

The holiday season reaches its climax on the night of December 24, which is called La Noche Buena, or The Good Night. Everyone attends midnight Mass and then gathers at home to celebrate, often all night long. They drink and dance, open presents, and eat specially prepared foods such as tamales

GREAT BALLS OF FIRE!

Every year, the city of Nejapa hosts one of the world's strangest—and possibly most dangerous—festivals: Bolas de Fuego *("Balls of Fire"). Legend has it that the tradition began after the eruption of the El Playon volcano in 1658—others say it was the eruption of 1922— when the volcano spit balls of fire into the air and forced the people of the village to flee. Another legend, or perhaps it is a variation on the same, says the town's patron saint, Saint Geronimo, fought the devil with fireballs.*

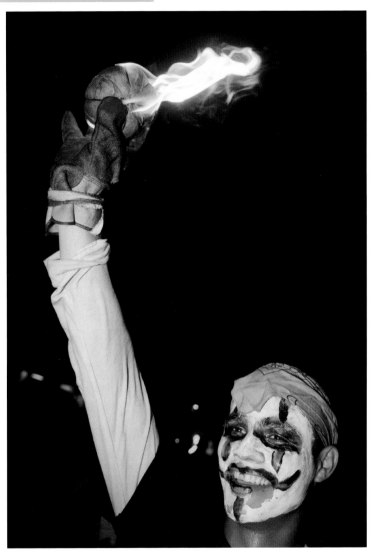

The festival is held on August 31. Two teams—good and evil—throw kerosene-soaked fireballs at each other. The balls are made of rags tied with wire and soaked for at least a month in advance. Players are typically young people in their teens and twenties who paint their faces and clothing for extra intrigue. Hundreds of bystanders cheer them on, and a good time is apparently had by all. Emergency personnel are on hand in case they are needed, which of course, they occasionally are. Astonishingly, however, there have been no reports of widespread disaster—so far.

and turkey. Salvadoran children receive their gifts from El Niño Dios, or Baby Jesus, on Christmas Eve.

People who can afford Christmas ornaments usually decorate lavishly. They often have a Christmas tree, but more common is the nativity scene, or *nacimiento* (na-see-mee-EN-toh), with statues or figurines that are often life-size. *Nacimientos* can be very elaborate, with farms and villages and little roads leading to the manger. People with fewer resources decorate a single small branch or dry bush to create their Christmas tree. Decorations are not taken down until January 6, the Day of the Three Kings, or Epiphany, which commemorates the day that the Three Kings finally arrived to see the baby Jesus after following the Star of Bethlehem.

New Year's Eve, December 31, is another occasion for festive eating, drinking, and dancing. Dinner typically consists of tamales and a roasted hen. However, it can also be a rather melancholy holiday, filled with hugging and crying as people ask pardon of their loved ones for the sins of the past year and promise to behave better in the coming year.

A girl dressed as a shepherdess takes part in a *pastorela*, a Christmas pageant, in Santo Tomas.

PATRON SAINTS' FESTIVALS

Because the Catholic Church has such a strong tradition in El Salvador, every city in the country has a patron saint, celebrated with a festival sometime during the year. The festivals usually last for an entire week and include a parade, soccer tournaments, and lots of eating, drinking, and dancing in the streets. The festivals are particularly colorful in native towns and villages; the celebrants dress up in their native costumes, with vivid plumage and colorful dress that is unique to their indigenous group. Their parade includes traditional indigenous dances and music. The biggest festival is held on August 6 for El Salvador del Mundo, or The Holy Savior of the World, patron saint of the whole country.

Catholics carry relics of Archbishop Oscar Romano during the San Salvador patron saint's day procession in August 2015.

INTERNET LINKS

www.bbc.com/news/world-latin-america-11172983
A short video shows some of the action at the Fireball Festival.

www.iexplore.com/travel-guides/central-and-south-america/el-salvador/festivals-and-events
This travel guide lists the main festivals in El Salvador.

www.suchitoto-el-salvador.com/english/cultura.htm
Sochitoto is a town in El Salvador with a wide variety of artistic and cultural festivals and events.

FOOD

A cook makes pupusas at a food stall.

13

A NATION'S FOODS REFLECT ITS history and natural environment. El Salvador's pre-Columbian heritage—the foods of the indigenous people—combined with Spanish tradition to create the country's cuisine today. It is hearty and basic, not spicy, and makes use of the fruits and vegetables that grow in the Central American climate—potatoes, yucca (cassava root), squashes, cabbage, carrots, onions, chipilín (a leafy green), tomatoes, peppers, plantains, bananas, pineapple, coconut, mangos, guavas, nance (a cherry-like fruit), and pacalla (palm flowers). In many ways, Salvadoran cooking is much like that of the other Central American countries, but even so, it has its own specialties.

The staple diet of most Salvadorans, especially in rural areas, is beans, rice, and tortillas, mainly because they cannot afford much more. Despite the high starch content of these staple foods, most Salvadorans

Sopa de pata is a popular Salvadoran soup or stew. It is typically made with cow feet, tripe (cow stomach), plantain, yucca, chayote, corn on the cob, onion, cabbage, green beans, and sometimes tomatoes and peppers. It is flavored with cilantro, garlic, and oregano.

only get about two-thirds of the calories they need, and malnutrition is one of the leading causes of death among the rural population. Meat, poultry, and fish are a rare treat. The choice of food available to wealthier city dwellers is much wider, and includes a variety of vegetables, fruit, poultry, and seafood. San Salvador is well known for its Chinese, French, and Italian restaurants, and for the abundance of excellent seafood; shrimp, lobster, and swordfish are all caught daily off El Salvador's coast. *Pupusas* (poo-POO-sas), the national fast food of filled tortillas, are sold at food stalls, markets, and small restaurants throughout El Salvador.

THE TYPICAL SALVADORAN DIET

In rural areas, people eat breakfast before the sun comes up, so the men can start working in the fields very early. Breakfast, or *desayuno* (de-sah-YOO-no), is a simple affair, consisting of coffee and a hot tortilla, which is sometimes diced and soaked in warm milk. Lunch, called *almuerzo* (al-mu-AIR-so), is the largest meal of the day. It typically consists of soup, with tortillas, rice, corn, or beans, and

A fishmonger shows off the day's catch at a market in La Libertad.

very occasionally meat, fish, or poultry. As in most Latin American countries, lunch usually lasts for about two hours, giving field workers a chance to rest before resuming work until dark. Dinner, or the *cena* (SAY-nah), is often a lighter meal, consisting of vegetables, tortillas, and beans.

For urban Salvadorans, breakfast usually consists of coffee, bread, and fruit. The midday meal is often tortillas with rice and beans and is not necessarily the largest meal of the day. Urban Salvadorans are not typically able to take a siesta in the middle of the day, unlike many other Latin Americans, although some shops do close for an hour or two at lunchtime. Families usually eat the evening meal together, which may include soup or vegetables, beans, rice, tortillas, and fish or meat. City supermarkets also provide a variety of processed foods imported from abroad.

TORTILLA MAKING

Making tortillas is considered to be the exclusive task of women. A woman starts making the day's supply of tortillas for her family early in the morning. The traditional method of making tortillas from scratch and by hand is still used by the typical rural woman.

First she must soak or boil the hard kernels of ripe corn in a mixture of water and white lime, which turns the corn into a starchy dough. She uses a handstone called a mano *(MAH-no) to grind the dough on a grinding stone, called a* metate *(may-TAH-tay). Then*

she kneads the dough by hand, slapping it back and forth between her hands until it forms a thin, round patty. When the tortillas are ready to be cooked, she fries them on a hot griddle, called a comal *(co-MAHL).*

DRINKS

Although coffee is El Salvador's primary export, the coffee served in El Salvador is often instant. Whether it is instant or brewed, it tends to be weak and bland. Salvadorans often dilute it with barley juice, and in rural areas, the taste is further altered by the necessity of adding bleach to the water to help prevent cholera. The most common cold drinks are *gaseosas* (ga-say-OH-sas), or sodas, and *refrescos* (ray-fres-KOS), which are fruit juices mixed with sugar and water.

IN THE KITCHEN

Kitchens in rural houses are usually located outside the house, either in a separate building or under a roof extending from the house. The women cook over a fire, or on a raised cement platform oven with a hollow center for the fire, over which they put a grill or griddle made of clay or metal. They must walk to a river or stream to fetch water, which they ration carefully throughout the day for their cooking and cleaning purposes.

Middle—and upper—class families, on the other hand, usually have at least one maid to help with cooking and cleaning. The maid will often do the shopping, although the *señora* (se-NYO-rah), or lady of the house, will usually prepare the list for her, and may even accompany her to the market. The *señora* also directs the daily menu, but the maid does most of the cooking. The kitchens in these houses are modern compared to rural kitchens, but they typically lack appliances such as dishwashers and washing machines because the maid cleans the dishes and often washes the clothes by hand.

Colorful juices are for sale at a fruit stall.

MARKETS

The traditional open-air market in El Salvador is crowded with close-set stalls offering a wide variety of goods: hot tortillas and tamales, handmade baskets, colorful flowers, fresh fruit and vegetables, live chickens or pigs, shoes, clothes, hammocks, and dishes. The air is full of rich aromas and noisy bargaining by women carrying netted handbags or large wicker baskets on their heads to hold their daily purchases. Shoppers thread their way through row upon row of fresh produce, including bananas, mangoes, melons, carrots, corn, avocadoes, cabbages, tomatoes, peppers, garlic, and potatoes. In the larger cities, modern supermarkets have supplanted some of the open-air markets, providing shoppers with an array of refrigerated, processed, and canned foods.

SALVADORAN SPECIALTIES

One of the most delicious and interesting foods is the *pupusa*, which is unique to El Salvador. *Pupusas* are small, thick corn tortillas filled with sausage, cheese, or beans and served hot, with salad or salsa. They are sold in *pupuserías* (poo-poo-say-REE-ah) all over El Salvador.

Tamales—steamed rolls of cornmeal stuffed with shredded meat, peppers, and corn and wrapped in corn husks—are another popular food, common to many Central American countries. Tamales take a great deal of time to prepare and are considered a dish for special occasions.

A favorite soup in El Salvador is *sopa de pata* (SOH-pah deh PAH-tah), or hoof soup, made from the hoof of a cow or an ox, with vegetables and sometimes beef tripe. *Sopa de pata* is made year-round, but it is especially popular during holidays and at family gatherings.

Homemade chicken and corn tamales are for special occasions.

INTERNET LINKS

www.whats4eats.com/central-america/el-salvador-cuisine
Whats4eats offers an excellent overview of Salvadoran cuisine with many recipes

www.who.int/features/2015/el-salvador-food-safety/en
This is a recent article from the World Health Organization about teaching food safety in El Salvador.

REFRESCO DE ENSALADA DE FRUTA (FRUIT SALAD JUICE)

Refrescos are popular fruit drinks.

1 ½ cups (360 mililiters) of chopped fresh
   pineapple, or 20 oz. can pineapple slices
   in pineapple juice
2 apples, unpeeled, finely chopped
2 oranges, peeled, finely chopped
juice from one freshly squeezed orange
juice from one lemon or lime
1 cup (240 ml) of mango, finely chopped
¼ cup (50 ml) of sugar
8 cups (2 liters) of cold water
a pinch of salt

Place chopped apples, oranges, mango,
and pineapple (with juice if using canned)
into a large bowl.

Add the lime and orange juice to fruit.

Add sugar, a pinch of salt, and stir.

Let the mixture sit for about 30 minutes to allow the flavors to blend.

Pour the fruit into a large pitcher (or two smaller pitchers) and add the water.

Stir and refrigerate for one hour.

This drink is best served fresh, but can be refrigerated for two days.

QUESADILLA SALVADOREÑA (SALVADORAN SWEET CHEESE POUNDCAKE)

Unlike the Mexican quesadilla, the Salvadoran *quesadilla* is a rich, sweet dessert cake often found in local *panaderías*, or bakeries.

2 cups (240 grams) flour
2 tsp baking powder
8 ounces (180 g) parmesan cheese, grated
2 cups (400 g) sugar
4 eggs, lightly beaten
1 cup (240 ml) whole milk
1 cup butter (240 ml), melted
2 Tbsp (32 g) sesame seeds (optional)

Preheat oven to 350°F (175°C).

Prepare two loaf pans with baking spray.

Sift the flour and baking powder together into a bowl. Set aside.

Combine the cheese, sugar, eggs, and milk in a large bowl and beat until smooth. Stir in the melted butter.

Slowly stir the flour mixture into the cheese mixture until fully incorporated and a smooth batter is formed.

Pour the batter into two well-greased loaf pans, filling them only halfway. If using, sprinkle the sesame seeds over the top of the batter.

Bake for 20 to 25 minutes, or until a toothpick inserted into the middle comes out clean. Set on racks and allow the cakes to come to room temperature before slicing and serving.

10 to 12 servings

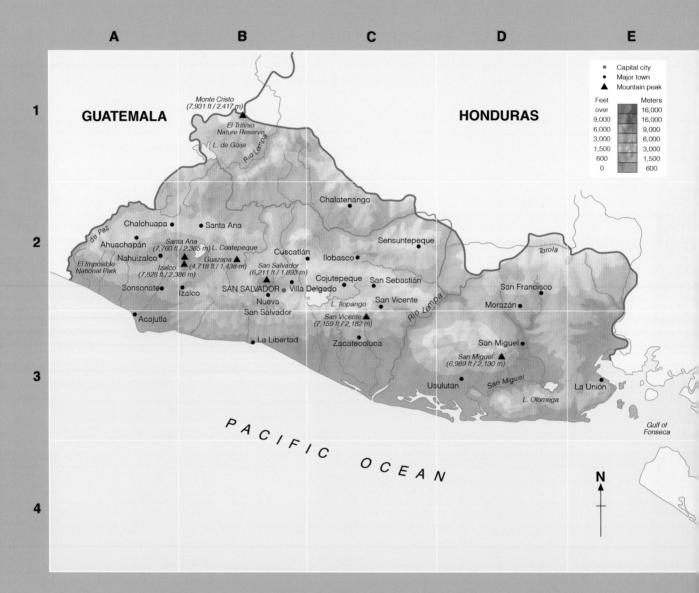

A　　　　　B　　　　　C　　　　　D　　　　　E

GUATEMALA　　　　　HONDURAS

- Capital city
- Major town
▲ Mountain peak

Feet		Meters
over		16,000
9,000		16,000
6,000		9,000
3,000		6,000
1,500		3,000
600		1,500
0		600

Monte Cristo
(7,931 ft / 2,417 m) ▲

El Trifinio
Nature Reserve

L. de Güija

Río Lempa

Chalatenango

Chalchuapa ● ● Santa Ana

de Paz

Sensuntepeque ●

Ahuachapán ●

Torola

Santa Ana
(7,760 ft / 2,365 m) L. Coatepeque

Nahuizalco ● Cuscatlán ● Ilobasco ●

El Imposible
National Park

Guazapa ▲
(4,718 ft / 1,438 m)

Izalco ▲
(7,828 ft / 2,386 m)

San Salvador
(6,211 ft / 1,893 m)

San Francisco ●

Sonsonate ● Izalco ● ▲

Cojutepeque ● San Sebastián ●

SAN SALVADOR ● Villa Delgado

Morazán ●

Nueva
San Salvador

San Vicente ●

Acajutla ●

L. Ilopango

San Vicente ▲
(7,159 ft / 2,182 m)

Río Lempa

San Miguel ●

La Libertad ●

Zacatecoluca ●

San Miguel ▲
(6,989 ft / 2,130 m)

Usulután ●

San Miguel

La Unión ●

L. Olomega

Gulf of
Fonseca

P A C I F I C   O C E A N

N

MAP OF EL SALVADOR

ECONOMIC EL SALVADOR

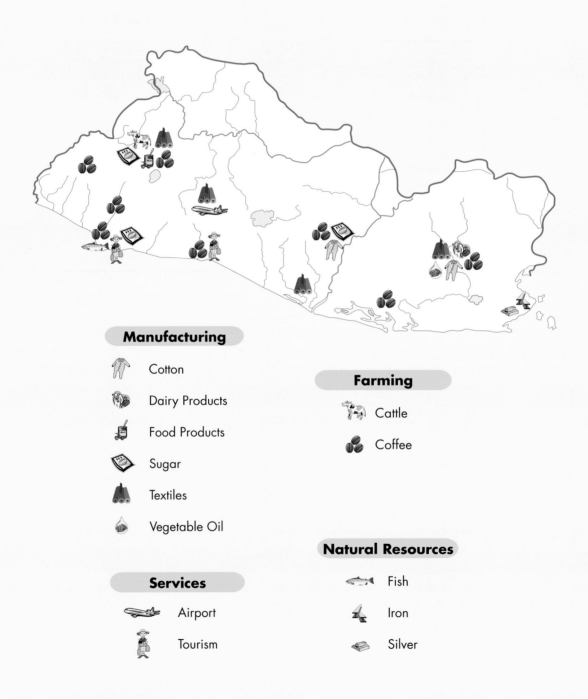

Manufacturing

- Cotton
- Dairy Products
- Food Products
- Sugar
- Textiles
- Vegetable Oil

Farming

- Cattle
- Coffee

Services

- Airport
- Tourism

Natural Resources

- Fish
- Iron
- Silver

ABOUT THE ECONOMY

GROSS DOMESTIC PRODUCT (GDP)
$50.94 billion (2014)

GDP PER CAPITA
$8,000 (2014)

GDP BY SECTOR
Agriculture 10 percent, industry 25.1 percent, services 64.9 percent (2014)

INFLATION
2 percent (2014)

INDUSTRIAL PRODUCTS
Processed food, beverages, petroleum, chemicals, fertilizer, textiles, furniture, light metals

AGRICULTURAL PRODUCTS
Coffee, sugar, corn, rice, beans, oilseed, cotton, sorghum, beef, dairy products

NATURAL RESOURCES
Hydropower, geothermal power, petroleum, land

CURRENCY
The US dollar is the legal tender in El Salvador.

WORKFORCE
2.752 million (2014)

WORKFORCE BY SECTOR
Agriculture 10 percent, industry 25 percent, services 65 percent (2014)

UNEMPLOYMENT RATE
5.5 percent with much underemployment (2014)

POPULATION BELOW POVERTY LINE
36.5 percent (2014)

EXTERNAL DEBT
$15.46 billion (2014)

PUBLIC DEBT
63.4 percent of GDP (2014)

EXPORTS
$4.521 billion (2014)

MAJOR EXPORTS
Offshore assembly exports, coffee, sugar, textiles, chemicals, electricity, gold

IMPORTS
$10.11 billion (2014)

MAJOR IMPORTS
Raw materials, consumer goods, capital goods, fuels, foodstuffs, petroleum, electricity

MAJOR TRADE PARTNERS
United States, Guatemala, Honduras, Mexico, China

CULTURAL EL SALVADOR

El Imposible National Park
This park is regarded as one of the last remaining tropical rain forests in El Salvador. It is home to such animals as puma, ocelot, and harpy eagle. The park's name comes from the Impossible Pass within it, which is a steep path that travellers used to traverse when passing through this forest.

El Trifinio Nature Reserve
This important conservation area is shared by three countries: El Salvador, Guatemala, and Honduras. Inside this reserve is the Monte Cristo cloud forest, one of the few remaining cloud forests in Central America.

Tazumal ruins
Located in Chalchuapa, near Santa Ana, this is the archaeological site of a 5000 BCE Mayan settlement. Tazumal in the Mayan language means "pyramid where the victims are burned." There is also a museum that displays artifacts found on the site.

San Salvador
El Salvador's capital is the largest city in the country and the second-largest in Central America. It has buildings of Spanish architectural design and is home to the National Theater and National Palace.

Lake Coatepeque
This beautiful lake is located at the foot of the Santa Ana volcano and is a popular recreation spot.

Santa Ana volcano
Santa Ana is the highest peak in El Salvador, rising to 7,749 feet (2,362 m). Its last eruption was in 1920.

Izalco volcano
Continuously active between 1700 until 1966, Izalco volcano was dubbed as the Lighthouse of the Pacific by seafarers in the nineteenth century. Molten lava running down its sides turned the volcano into a brightly glowing beacon that could be seen miles out to sea.

Lake Ilopango
El Salvador's largest lake fills the crater of an extinct volcano. It is located at an altitude of 1,450 feet (442 m) and has a surface area of 40 square miles (100 square km). The lake is a popular resort and tourist area.

San Andrés ruins
This site in La Libertad was a ceremonial center of the Mayan civilization. It was inhabited by a succession of Maya, Aztec, and Pipil.

Joya De Cerén ruins
The farming community at this site in La Libertad was buried by a volcanic eruption in 600 CE, which preserves the remains in excellent condition. Artifacts and structures provide good insights into the residents' daily lives. Joya de Cerén is a UNESCO World Heritage Site.

COUNTRY NAME

Republic of El Salvador; Short form, El Salvador. Note: name is an abbreviation of the original Spanish conquistador designation for the area *Provincia de Nuestro Senor Jesus Cristo, el Salvador del Mundo* ("Province of Our Lord Jesus Christ, the Saviour of the World"), which became simply El Salvador ("The Savior")

NATIONAL FLAG

Three equal horizontal bands of blue, white, and blue with the national coat of arms in the center of the white band; the coat of arms features a round emblem encircled by the words "Republica de El Salvador en la America Central."

NATIONAL ANTHEM

"Himno Nacional de El Salvador" (National Anthem of El Salvador), composed by Juan Aberle and lyrics by General Juan José Cañas. Adopted as the national anthem in 1879 and officially recognized in 1953.

CAPITAL

San Salvador

OTHER MAJOR CITIES

Santa Ana, San Miguel
Administrative Departments
Fourteen departments: Ahuachapan, Cabanas, Chalatenango, Cuscatlán, La Libertad, La Paz, La Unión, Morazán, San Miguel, San Salvador, Santa Ana, San Vicente, Sonsonate, Usulután

POPULATION

6,141,350 (2015)

ETHNIC GROUPS

Mestizo 86.3 percent, white 12.7 percent, Amerindian .2 percent, black .1 percent

LIFE EXPECTANCY

Men 71.14 years, women 77.86 years (2015)

LITERACY RATE

Men 90.4 percent, women 86 percent (2015)

OFFICIAL LANGUAGE

Spanish

MAJOR RELIGION

Roman Catholicism

LEADERS IN POLITICS

Chief of State: President Salvador Sánchez Cerén (since June 1, 2014); Vice President Salvador Óscar Ortiz (since June 1, 2014)

TIMELINE

IN EL SALVADOR	IN THE WORLD
	753 BCE Rome is founded.
500 BCE Early Mayan civilization	**116–117 CE** The Roman Empire reaches its greatest extent, under Emperor Trajan.
600–900 CE Height of Mayan civilization	
900–1200 Mayan civilization declines.	**1000** The Chinese perfect gunpowder and begin to use it in warfare.
1524 Spanish conquistador Pedro de Alvarado leads troops to attack El Salvador in search of gold and silver. Natives put up resistance.	**1530** Beginning of transatlantic slave trade organized by the Portuguese in Africa.
1540 Natives overcome by disease, slavery, and weapon shortage. El Salvador becomes a Spanish colony.	**1558–1603** Reign of Elizabeth I of England **1620** Pilgrims sail the *Mayflower* to America. **1776** US Declaration of Independence **1789–1799** The French Revolution
1821 Independence from Spain	
1823 El Salvador becomes part of the United Provinces of Central America.	
1840 El Salvador becomes fully independent.	
1859–1863 President Gerardo Barrios introduces coffee-growing.	**1861** The US Civil War begins. **1869** The Suez Canal is opened. **1914** World War I begins.
1932 A peasant uprising led by Agustine Farabundo Marti leads to thirty thousand people being killed during the suppression.	**1939** World War II begins.

IN EL SALVADOR	IN THE WORLD
	1945 World War II ends.
	1957 The Russians launch *Sputnik*.
1969 The Soccer War with Honduras.	**1966–1969** The Chinese Cultural Revolution
1980 Archbishop Óscar Romero assassinated. José Napoleón Duarte becomes president.	
1981 Massacre of El Mozote.	
	1986 Nuclear power disaster at Chernobyl in Ukraine
1992 Government and FMLN sign peace accord. FMLN recognized as political party.	**1991** Break-up of the Soviet Union
1993 Government declares amnesty for those implicated in human rights atrocities.	**1997** Hong Kong is returned to China.
1998 Hurricane Mitch kills 374 Salvadorans.	
2001 El Salvador adopts US dollar as national currency. Earthquakes kill 1,400 people.	**2001** Terrorists crash planes in New York, Washington, DC, and Pennsylvania.
2004 ARENA candidate Tony Saca wins presidential elections.	**2003** War in Iraq.
	2008 Barack Obama is elected US president.
2014 Salvador Sánchez Cerén of FMLN becomes president.	
2015 Beatification of Archbishop Óscar Romero celebrated in San Salvador.	**2015** Cuba and United States re-establish diplomatic relations.

GLOSSARY

brujería (brew-hay-REE-ya)
Witchcraft that is really a form of native medicine practiced in some rural areas.

choza (CHO-sah)
A rural house made of woven branches and covered with mud.

coup
The removal of a government, illegally and by force, usually by the military.

curandero (cur-ahn-DE-roh)
An indigenous witch doctor or healer.

Cuscatlán
The native name for the region that now includes El Salvador. It means "Land of the Jewel."

gaseosa (ga-say-OH-sah)
Soft drink

junta
A small group ruling a country, especially after a coup and before a legal government has been elected.

machismo
Latin American ideal of manliness.

madrino (ma-DREE-no)
Godmother

matanza (mah-TAN-zah)
Massacre or slaughter

mesones (may-SON-ays)
Single-story buildings, usually run-down, consisting of a connected series of small, individual dwellings, surrounding a common courtyard.

mestizo
A person of mixed European and native ancestry.

Nahua
Language of the Pipil.

oligarchy
A small group of people exercising political control, usually for corrupt and selfish purposes.

padrino (pa-DREE-no)
Godfather

pupusa (poo-POO-sah)
A thick corn tortilla filled with beans, meat, or cheese; a special dish of El Salvador.

pupusería (poo-poo-say-REE-ah)
A restaurant or food stall where pupusa is sold.

tugurios (tu-GU-ryos)
Shantytowns

FOR FURTHER INFORMATION

BOOKS

Danner, Mark. *The Massacre at El Mozote*. New York: Vintage, 1994.

Frazier, Joseph P. *El Salvador Could Be Like That: A Memoir of War, Politics and Journalism on the Front-Row of the Last Bloody Conflict of the US-Soviet Cold War*. Ojai, Calif.: Karina Library Press, 2013.

Stout, Anna M. *El Salvador: Lessons on Love and Resilience*. Grand Junction, Colo.: Foundation for Cultural Exchange, 2014.

DVDS/FILMS

Chronic Neglect: The Water Crisis in El Salvador. CDC / WITNESS, 2011.

Innocent Voices. Lightyear Video, 2008.

Maria's Story: A Documentary Portrait of Love And Survival In El Salvador's Civil War. PM Press, 2010.

Monsenor: The Last Journey of Oscar Romero. First Run Features, 2012.

Romero. Vision Video, 2009.

MUSIC

Los Hermanos Lovo. *¡Soy Salvadoreño! Chanchona Music from Eastern El Salvador*. Washington, DC: Smithsonian Folkways, 2011.

Peter, Paul and Mary. "El Salvador." *No Easy Walk to Freedom*. Burbank, Calif.: Warner Bros. 1992 original release; 2008.

Pipil Indians of El Salvador, The. Washington, DC: Folkways Records, 2012.

ONLINE

BBC News. El Salvador Country Profile. news.bbc.co.uk/2/hi/americas/country_profiles/1220684.stm

CIA World Factbook. El Salvador. www.cia.gov/library/publications/the-world-factbook/geos/es.html

Lonely Planet. El Salvador. www.lonelyplanet.com/el-salvador

New York Times, The. Times Topics: El Salvador. topics.nytimes.com/top/news/international/countriesandterritories/elsalvador/index.html

New York Times, The. "Killed in El Salvador." (video) www.nytimes.com/video/us/100000003224677/a-search-for-justice.html

BIBLIOGRAPHY

BOOKS and websites

BBC News. El Salvador profile — Timeline. www.bbc.com/news/world-latin-america-19402222

Carrillo, Carlos Velásquez. "Do the '14 Families' Still Exist? Is There Even Still an Oligarchy?" *Envio*, July 2009. www.envio.org.ni/articulo/4031

CIA World Factbook. El Salvador. www.cia.gov/library/publications/the-world-factbook/geos/es.html

Ertil, Randy Jurado. "Is El Salvador Heading to a Second Civil War?" *Huffington Post*, July 24, 2015. www.huffingtonpost.com/randy-jurado/is-el-salvador-heading-to_b_7858680.html

Grillo, Ioan. "Inside El Salvador's 'War Without Sense'." *Time*, July 24, 2015. time.com/3966900/el-salvador-gangs-violence

Index Mundi. El Salvador—International Tourism. www.indexmundi.com/facts/el-salvador/international-tourism

Kahn, Carrie. "In El Salvador, Gang Killings Take An Agonizing Toll." NPR, July 12, 2015. www.npr.org/sections/parallels/2015/07/12/422059575/in-el-salvador-gang-killings-take-an-agonizing-toll

Karunananthan, Meera. "The human right to water: Salvadoran NGOs and a global campaign." *The Guardian*, March 25, 2015. www.theguardian.com/global-development-professionals-network/2015/mar/25/human-right-water-salvadoran-ngos-global-campaign

Lonely Planet. El Salvador. www.lonelyplanet.com/el-salvador

Migration Policy Institute. "The Salvadoran Diaspora in the United States." June 2105 revised.

Negroponte, Diana Villiers. "Remembering El Salvador's Peace Accord: Why Was That Peace Elusive?" Upfront, The Brookings Institution, January 19, 2012. www.brookings.edu/blogs/up-front/posts/2012/01/19-el-salvador-negroponte

Partlow, Joshua. "El Salvador is on pace to become the hemisphere's most deadly nation." *The Washington Post*, May 17, 2015. www.washingtonpost.com/world/the_americas/el-salvador-is-on-pace-to-become-the-hemispheres-most-deadly-nation/2015/05/17/fc52e4b6-f74b-11e4-a47c-e56f4db884ed_story.html

Paulson, Tom. "El Salvador fights to protect its water and people from 'free trade.'" Humanosphere, April 15, 2015. www.humanosphere.org/environment/2015/04/el-salvador-is-fighting-to-protect-its-water-from-free-trade

US Department of State, Bureau of Consular Affairs, US Passports and International Travel. "El Salvador Travel Warning." June 22, 2015. travel.state.gov/content/passports/english/alertswarnings/el-salvador-travel-warning.html

US Department of State, Bureau of Western Hemisphere Affairs, "US Relations with El Salvador." July 29, 2015.

Watson, Katy. "How gang violence is spreading fear in El Salvador." BBC News, May 29, 2015. www.bbc.com/news/world-latin-america-32913749

INDEX

INDEX